中国思想文化术语多语种对外翻译
标准化建设项目成果
CHINESE THINKING AND CULTURE
MULTILINGUAL TERMINOLOGY DATABASE

中华源·河南故事
CHINESE CIVILIZATION
Stories from Henan

庄子
ZHUANGZI

河南省人民政府外事办公室　编

河南大学出版社
HENAN UNIVERSITY PRESS
·郑州·

图书在版编目（CIP）数据

中华源·河南故事. 庄子：汉、英 / 河南省人民政府外事办公室编. -- 郑州：河南大学出版社，2021.4
ISBN 978-7-5649-4619-7

Ⅰ. ①中… Ⅱ. ①河… Ⅲ. ①地方文化 - 河南 - 通俗读物 - 汉、英②庄周（约前369- 前286）- 传记 - 通俗读物 - 汉、英 Ⅳ. ①G127.61-49②B223.5-49

中国版本图书馆CIP数据核字（2021）第069935号

责任编辑	孙增科
责任校对	屈琳玉
封面设计	翟淼淼
出版发行	河南大学出版社
	地址：郑州市郑东新区商务外环中华大厦2401号　邮编：450046
	电话：0371-86059701（营销部）
	0371-86059750（高等教育与职业教育分公司）
	网址：hupress.henu.edu.cn
排　　版	河南大学出版社设计排版部
印　　刷	河南博雅彩印有限公司
版　　次	2021年4月第1版　　　　印　次　2021年4月第1次印刷
开　　本	710 mm×1010 mm　1/16　印　张　11
字　　数	176千　　　　　　　　　定　价　56.00元

版权所有，侵权必究
本书如有印装质量问题，请与河南大学出版社营销部联系调换。

"中华源·河南故事"系列丛书编委会

顾　　问	黄友义　杨　平　范大祺
名誉主任	穆为民　何金平　刘炯天
主　　任	付　静
副 主 任	陈　岩　陈志伟　刁玉华　方启雄　介晓磊
	孔留安　李冰冰　李向前　李　镇　梁留科
	刘金锋　牛卫国　屈鹏飞　史永庆　田　凯
	万正峰　王建修　王清义　王自文　许二平
	杨建伟　杨玮斌　张改平　张俊峰　张明超
	张松文　赵卫东
主　　编	付　静
副 主 编	李冰冰
编　　委	陈玮　丁锐　高阳　徐恒振　郑延保

中华源·河南故事·庄子

主　　编	介晓磊
副 主 编	李可亭　周运增（英文）
中文撰稿	刘洪生　陈功文
英文译者	杨　静
英文审校	〔美〕Zachariah M Randolph
绘　　图	严琰　吴姝然

The Editorial Committee
Chinese Civilization
Stories from Henan

Consultants	Huang Youyi Yang Ping Fan Daqi
Honorary Directors	Mu Weimin He Jinping Liu Jiongtian
Director	Fu Jing
Deputy Directors	Chen Yan Chen Zhiwei Diao Yuhua Fang Qixiong Jie Xiaolei Kong Liu'an Li Bingbing Li Xiangqian Li Zhen Liang Liuke Liu Jinfeng Niu Weiguo Qu Pengfei Shi Yongqing Tian Kai Wan Zhengfeng Wang Jianxiu Wang Qingyi Wang Ziwen Xu Erping Yang Jianwei Yang Weibin Zhang Gaiping Zhang Junfeng Zhang Mingchao Zhang Songwen Zhao Weidong
Chief Editor	Fu Jing
Deputy Chief Editor	Li Bingbing
Editors	Chen Wei Ding Rui Gao Yang Xu Hengzhen Zheng Yanbao

Chinese Civilization
Stories from Henan
Zhuangzi

Editor-in-Chief	Jie Xiaolei
Associate Editors-in-Chief	Li Keting Zhou Yunzeng (English Text)
Writers	Liu Hongsheng Chen Gongwen
English Translator	Yang Jing
Translation Proofreader	Zachariah M Randolph (U.S.)
Illustrators	Yan Yan Wu Shuran

总　序

中国是世界四大文明古国之一,也是世界上唯一的古代文明传统未曾中断的国家。河南省地处中国中东部,是中华文明和中华民族的重要发祥地,在中国五千年的文明史上,河南作为国家政治、经济、文化的中心就长达三千多年。从某种意义上讲,一部河南史就是半部中国史。这里是中华人文始祖黄帝的故乡,是古丝绸之路的东方起点,是少林功夫和陈氏太极的发源地,这里创建了中国历史上最早的都城,镌刻了中国最古老的文字,诞生了中国最初的商业文明。

伴随着新时代的荣光,河南经济社会发展迅速,人民生活水平显著提升,这是河南人民自力更生、艰苦奋斗的历史结果,也是对外开放带来的益处。河南经济社会的发展、人民生活方式的改变都植根于深层次的文化积淀。为了让世界更多地了解河南,让河南更好地走向世界,2018年以来,河南省人民政府外事办公室认真研析了这片古老土地上的历史文化资源和时代风貌,组织各领域权威专家学者,编译了"中华源·河南故事"中外文系列丛书,选取黄河文化、河洛文化、老子、庄子、黄帝、少林功夫、太极拳、中医、汉字、丝绸之路、古都、农业、大运河、文物、陶瓷、青铜器、手工艺、书法、杂技、豫菜、豫剧、脱贫攻坚、空中丝绸之路、航空城、南水北调、中国粮谷、红旗渠、焦裕禄等多个主题,力图以故事的方式向世界展现一个立体、全面、真实的河南。

当今世界,人类文明无论是在物质还是在精神方面都取得了巨大进步,特别是物质的极大丰富,这在古代世界是完全不能想象的。同时,当代人类也面临着许多突出的难题，比如，贫富差距持续扩大，物欲追求奢华无度，个人主义恶性膨胀，社会诚信不断消减，伦理道德每况愈下，人与自然关系日趋紧张，等等。要解决这些难题，不仅需要运用人类今天的智慧和力量，而且需要运用人类历史上积累和储存的智慧和力量。河南历史文化底蕴深厚、包容性强，在今天仍极具现实意义。中原文化蕴含的思想智慧有助于修身养性，推动人类社会进步发展，焦裕禄精神、红旗渠精神所体现的为民爱民、艰苦奋斗的价值取向是构建人类命运共同体的力量源泉。我们期待与读者们一起从河南故事中汲取更多的智慧和力量，共同创造更加美好的未来。

Series Foreword

China is one of the four ancient civilizations in the world, and is also the only country in the world where the ancient civilization has not been interrupted. Located in east-central China, Henan Province is an important cradle for the Chinese nation and Chinese civilization. In the course of the five thousand years of Chinese history, for more than three thousand years it served as the political, economic and cultural center of the country and therefore, as generally accepted, represents half of the history of China. Henan is the native place of Yellow Emperor, the cradle of Chinese culture, the starting point of the ancient Silk Road in the east, and the birthplace of Shaolin Kungfu and Chen-style Taijiquan—typical examples of the world-renowned Chinese martial arts. It was here that the earliest capital city in China was founded, the oldest Chinese characters engraved, and the earliest commerce took shape.

In the new era, Henan has witnessed rapid growth in its economy and remarkable improvement of people's living conditions owing to the national reform and opening-up policy and unremitting endeavors of the people. Modern economic achievements and social development as well as the changes of way of life could be traced back to its traditional values and cultural heritages. To enable people from other countries to understand Henan, and let the Province integrate more efficiently into the world development, the Foreign Affairs Office of the People's Government of Henan Province has organized teams of authoritative experts and scholars in relevant fields to compile this *Chinese Civilization: Stories from Henan* in Chinese and foreign languages since 2018 by crystallizing the excellence of traditions and outstanding features of modern development. The book series include *The Yellow River Culture*, *Heluo Culture*, *Laozi*, *Zhuangzi*, *The Yellow Emperor*, *Shaolin Kungfu*, *Taijiquan*, *Traditional Chinese Medicine*, *Chinese Characters*, *The Silk Road*, *Ancient Chinese Capitals*, *Feeding the*

People—Agriculture, *The Grand Canal*, *Cultural Heritage*, *Ceramic*, *Bronze*, *Handicraft Art*, *Calligraphy*, *Acrobatics*, *Henan Cuisine*, *Henan Opera*, *Poverty Alleviation*, *Silk Road in the Air*, *Zhengzhou—An Aviation City*, *South-to-North Water Diversion*, *China Grain Valley*, *Man-Made River—Hongqiqu Canal*, *A Model Official—Jiao Yulu*, etc., presenting a panoramic picture of the Province.

In today's world, human civilization has made great progress in both material accumulation and ethical advancement, and the great abundance of materials today, especially, is beyond the imagination of the ancient people. At the same time, however, modern people are also confronted with a lot of problems, such as the widening gap between the rich and the poor, the indulgence in pursuit of luxury and extravagance, the undesirable extension of individualism, the decline of social integrity, and the increasingly tense relationship between man and nature. To solve the problems, we need to draw on the wisdom and powers developed today as well as those accumulated in the past. Henan is endowed with rich historical and cultural heritages characterized by its inclusiveness, and such heritages remain significant today. The intelligence and wisdom in Henan culture are conducive to self-cultivation and to the promotion of social development. The spirit of serving the people and relentless struggle, as embodied in Jiao Yulu and Man-Made River—Hongqiqu Canal provides source of strength for building a community with a shared future for mankind. It is our hope that wisdom and strength from Henan stories could lead us to a shared brilliant future.

前　言

庄子，本名庄周，字子休，战国时期宋国蒙（今河南商丘）人，与孟子、梁惠王生活在同一时期。

庄子生于动荡不安的年代，也是宋国灭亡前最为黑暗混乱的时期，同时也正值诸子百家争鸣的时代。不同思想相互交锋，影响了当时每一个人，庄子也不例外。他的生活与一般老百姓一样，有妻有子，努力在乱世中苟全性命。但他博览群书，深谙人情世故，领悟高明智慧，自有一套人生哲学。庄子坚守自己的理想，保持本真，安贫乐道，藐视荣华富贵，独守超然世外的生活。他为了谋生，曾短期为官，做过蒙的小官漆园吏。中年以后，他的生活极为贫困，住在穷街陋巷，织鞋为生，常常饿得面黄肌瘦，由此而了解到下层人民的生活状况。

庄子是继老子李耳之后道家学派又一代表人物，大体上继承了老子的学说，并对老子思想有所发展。老子讲"天道"，倡"无为"，庄子也谈"天道"，宣扬"无为"。这是老庄思想的核心。但庄子并非仅仅对老子思想进行发挥，他谈"逍遥"、论"齐物"、说"养生"，都有独到的见解，并形成了个性鲜明的哲学和艺术特色。后世将庄子与老子并称为"老庄"，他们的哲学思想体系，被称为"老庄哲学"。

庄子最重要的思想是无为、无己，完成天地间一番逍遥游，独与天地精神往来，与世间万物一体。与看重人的社会属性、带有强烈的政治伦理色彩的儒家学说相比，庄子思想则是一种重视人的自然本性、关怀人的生命和精神的学说。庄子自然人本精神首先体现在对生命的热爱和珍惜上，带有一种强烈的个性色彩，在儒家思想为主导的封建社会，庄子的自然人本精神对中国文人独立人格的养成，起着不可忽视的作用。

庄子不但是中国哲学史上一位著名的思想家，同时也是中国文学史上一位杰出的文学家。《庄子》一书，标志着在战国时期中国的哲学思想和文学语言已经发展到非常高的水平，是中国古代典籍中的瑰宝。在3—5世纪的魏晋时期，《庄子》和《周易》《老子》一起并称"三玄"，对当时的哲学思想产生了重大影响。

《庄子》是继《老子》之后的又一部体现道家思想的著作，是中国古老的哲学原典之一，在唐代被尊为《南华真经》。书中不仅充满了哲思，而且想象奇幻，构思巧妙，语言生动优美，富有诗情画意，充满了浓厚的文学色彩，达到了哲理性与文学性的完美结合，是先秦诸子文章的典范之作。庄子还在书中虚构了众多光怪陆离、丰富多彩的寓言故事，幽默诙谐，瑰丽诡谲，给人以启迪，是浪漫主义文学的杰作。鲁迅在《汉文学史纲要》中评价庄子的文章："汪洋辟（捭）阖，仪态万方，晚周诸子之作，莫能先也。"可谓至言。

《庄子》在思想、艺术方面对后世产生了很大的影响。作为道家的原典，该书与儒家原典一起参与了中华民族独特性格、思维方式、处事方式的塑造。《庄子》浪漫的风格和独特的审美思想，影响了一代又一代人，汉代的贾谊、司马迁，唐代诗人李白、李贺，宋代大文豪苏轼，清代小说家曹雪芹等都从《庄子》中汲取了丰富的营养。而书中的寓言故事，更是对后世小说产生了巨大的影响，被誉为"千百世诙谐小说之祖"（宋代黄震《黄氏日抄》）。书中的语言演变成成语流传至今的有很多，如"望洋兴叹""东施效颦""朝三暮四""运斤成风""得意忘言"等，都为我们所熟知。郭沫若充分肯定了《庄子》的影响，他说，秦汉以来的中国文学史差不多大半是在《庄子》的影响下发展的（《鲁迅与庄子》），可见庄子的地位与影响。即使在当代，《庄子》对当代文化的建构也有巨大作用。

《庄子》这本先秦道家典籍在海外也很受欢迎，成了世界文化遗产。19世纪末期,英国著名作家奥斯卡·王尔德曾说:"我在《庄子》一书中看到了一种我从来未遇到过的对现代生活的最尖锐和最苛刻的批评";"那些对中国文化略知皮毛的人如果认真读一读《庄子》,一定吃惊得发抖的"。到了现代,英国李约瑟、日本汤川秀树、美国卡普拉等人,形成了一个国际性的道家新学派。

目前,《庄子》在世界各地有多种语言的注本和译本出版发行,流传较广。无论东亚的日本、朝鲜,还是欧美国家,都有多种关于《庄子》的注本和译本在流传。甚至连一些欧洲小国家也有自己的《庄子》译本,如瑞典、波兰、匈牙利等国。《庄子》在海外的流传与影响,对于促进中外文化交流,让世界了解中国文化,有十分重要的意义。

本书编写组　2021年1月

Preface

Zhuangzi, whose real name is Zhuang Zhou and the courtesy name is Zixiu, was born in the region of Meng in the state of Song (now Shangqiu, Henan Province) during the period of Warring States. He lived in the same period as Mencius and King Hui of the State of Liang.

Zhuangzi was born in a turbulent era, which was also the most dark and chaotic period before the fall of the state of Song. At the same time, it was also an era of contention among a hundred schools of thought. Different ideas clashed with each other, affecting everyone at that time, and Zhuangzi was no exception. His life was the same as that of ordinary people who had a family and tried to survive in troubled times. However, he was well read, well versed in worldly wisdom, and had his own philosophy of life. Zhuangzi held fast to his ideal, kept his true nature, lived in peace and contentment, despised honor and wealth, and lived in a detached life. In order to make a living, he had been an official for a short time, a small official in lacquer-yard in his hometown of Meng. After middle age, he lived in extreme poverty, living in poor streets and alleys, weaving shoes for a living, often hungry and skinny, from which he learned about the living conditions of the people in lower class.

Zhuangzi is another representative of Taoist school after Laozi (Li Er). He mainly inherits Laozi's thought and develops it. Laozi advocates "Tiantao (the way of heaven)" and "Wuwei (Inaction)", and Zhuangzi also does so. The above is the core of Laozi and Zhuangzi's thoughts. But Zhuangzi is not confined to the thought of Laozi; instead, he forms his own distinctive philosophical thought and artistic characteristics by advocating "Absolute Freedom", "Taking All Things Equal" and "Health Preservation". Later generations call Zhuangzi and Laozi "Lao Zhuang", and their philosophical system is called "Lao Zhuang philosophy".

The most important thought of Zhuangzi is inaction(to do nothing), to have no self, to complete a free and easy wandering between heaven and earth, to immerse into the spirit of heaven and earth alone, and to integrate with all things in the world. Compared with Confucianism, which values human's social attribute and maintains strong political and ethical color, the thought of Zhuangzi is a theory which attaches importance to human's inborn nature and cares for human's life and spirit. The natural humanistic spirit of Zhuangzi firstly embodies his love and treasure of life, with a strong personality. In the feudal society dominated by Confucianism, Zhuangzi's natural humanistic spirit plays an important role in the cultivation of Chinese scholar's independent personality.

Zhuangzi is not only a famous thinker in the history of Chinese philosophy, but also an outstanding writer in the history of Chinese literature. *Zhuangzi* (*The Book of Master Zhuang*) marks that in the Warring States period, Chinese philosophy and literary language have developed to a very high level, which is a treasure in ancient Chinese classics. In the Wei Jin period between the 3rd and 5th century, *Zhuangzi*, *Zhouyi* (*Book of Changes*) and *Laozi* (*Tao Te Ching*) were called "Three Metaphysical Classics" together, which had a great influence on the philosophy at that time.

Zhuangzi is another work reflecting Taoism after Laozi. It is one of the ancient philosophical classics in China which is honored as *The Holy Canon of Nanhua* in the Tang Dynasty. The book is not only full of philosophical thinking, but also imaginative fantasy, ingenious conception, vivid and beautiful language, poetic and idyllic mood, and strong literary color. These qualities together achieve the perfect combination of philosophy and literary, and is a model in the works of pre-Qin scholars. Zhuangzi also makes up many strange and colorful fables in the book, which are humorous and magnificent, changeable and enlightening. It is a masterpiece of romantic literature. Lu Xun commented on Zhuangzi's work in *The Outline of the History of Chinese Literature*, "His prose is marvelous and elegant in numerous styles. No other works of hundred schools in late Zhou Dynasty can be compared." It's true.

Zhuangzi has been exerting great influence on later generations. As the original canon of Taoism, the book, together with the original canon of Confucianism, takes part in the shaping of the unique character, way of thinking and way of doing things of the Chinese nation. The romantic style and unique aesthetic thought of *Zhuangzi* have influenced Chinese people generation after generation. Jia Yi and Sima Qian of the Han Dynasty, Li Bai and Li He of the Tang Dynasty, Su Shi of the Song Dynasty and Cao Xueqin of the Qing Dynasty all are influenced deeply by *Zhuangzi*. The fables in the book have a great influence on later novels, and are known as the "ancestor of thousands of humorous novels" (*Huang's Daily Writing* by Huang Zhen of the Song Dynasty) . The language in the book has been evolved into idioms, and many of them have been handed down to the present day. These idioms have amazing expressions, such as "Sighing to the Sea", "Dongshi Imitating Xishi", "Three at Dusk and Four at Dawn" , "Whirling Axe with Noise Like Wind" and "Meaning Grasped but Language Forgotten" which are well known to us. Guo Moruo fully affirmed the influence of *Zhuangzi* on the development of Chinese literature since the Qin and Han dynasties (*Luxun and Zhuangzi*), which showed the important status of *Zhuangzi*. Even in the contemporary era, *Zhuangzi* plays a great role in the construction of contemporary culture.

Zhuangzi, a Taoist classic of pre-Qin period, is also popular abroad and has become a world cultural heritage. At the end of the 19th century, Oscar Wilde, a famous British writer, once said, "I saw the sharpest and harshest criticism of modern life from *Zhuangzi*, which I had never met before." "Those who have superficial knowledge of Chinese culture will be shocked if they read *Zhuangzi* seriously." In modern times, Joseph Needham of England, Hideki Yukawa of Japan and Kapra of America had formed an international new school of Taoism.

At present, annotated versions and translated versions of *Zhuangzi* have been published in many languages all over the world. There are various versions of *Zhuangzi* spreading in both East Asian countries of Japan, Korea, and American and European countries. Even some small countries have their own versions of *Zhuangzi*, such as Sweden, Poland, Hungary and so on. The spread and influence of *Zhuangzi* abroad is of great significance to promote cultural exchanges between China and other countries, and establish the status of Chinese culture in the world culture.

The writer group, January 2021

目 录　　Contents

第一章　庄子其人　　001
　　一、宋国蒙人　　002
　　二、做官漆园吏　　008
　　三、钓于濮水　　012
　　四、庄子与惠施　　014
　　五、庄子之墓　　018

Chapter 1　An Introduction to Zhuangzi　　001
　　Ⅰ. From the State of Song　　003
　　Ⅱ. Being an Official in Lacquer-yard　　009
　　Ⅲ. Fishing on the Pu River　　013
　　Ⅳ. Zhuangzi and Huishi　　015
　　Ⅴ. The Tomb of Zhuangzi　　019

第二章　庄子的思想学说　　023
　　一、宇宙观　　024
　　二、认识论　　028
　　三、人生观　　032
　　四、政治观　　036
　　五、美学观与文艺观　　038

Chapter 2　The Theory and Thought of Zhuangzi　　023
　　Ⅰ. Cosmology　　025
　　Ⅱ. Epistemology　　029
　　Ⅲ. View of Life　　033
　　Ⅳ. Political Views　　037

Ⅴ. Aesthetic and Literary Views　　039

第三章　庄子的文学艺术特色　047
　　一、寓言、重言、卮言　　048
　　二、庄子散文的艺术特色　　052

Chapter 3　The Literary and Artistic Characteristics of Zhuangzi　047
　　Ⅰ. Fables, Quoted and Random Talks　　049
　　Ⅱ. The Artistic Features of Proses in Zhuangzi　　053

第四章　庄子的历史地位及影响　063
Chapter 4　The Literary and Artistic Characteristics of Zhuangzi　063

第五章　庄子寓言50则　073
　　1. 鹏程万里　　074
　　2. 丽姬悔泣　　074
　　3. 鼓盆而歌　　074
　　4. 庄周梦蝶　　076
　　5. 邯郸学步　　078
　　6. 越俎代庖　　078
　　7. 朝三暮四　　080
　　8. 魍魉问影　　082
　　9. 庖丁解牛　　082
　　10. 望洋兴叹　　084
　　11. 浑沌开窍　　086
　　12. 不材之木　　086
　　13. 藐姑射山神人　　088
　　14. 螳臂当车　　090
　　15. 呆若木鸡　　092
　　16. 东施效颦　　094

17.螳螂捕蝉	096
18.运斤成风	096
19.濠梁观鱼	098
20.探骊得珠	100
21.得鱼忘筌	100
22.鹓雏腐鼠	102
23.蛮触之争	104
24.大钩巨缁	104
25.智有所困	106
26.轮扁斫轮	108
27.坎井之蛙	108
28.庄子借粮	110
29.天机所动	112
30.舐痔得车	112
31.大小之别	114
32.不龟手之药	116
33.许由辞帝位	118
34.大瓠无用	120
35.秦失吊丧	120
36.支离疏养生	122
37.无趾务学	122
38.子桑思贫	124
39.盗也有道	126
40.吕梁丈夫	126
41.云将东游	128
42.削木为镱	130
43.桓公见鬼	132
44.老汉粘蝉	134

45. 举鲁儒服	136
46. 弄水浸畦	138
47. 白驹过隙	138
48. 肘上生瘤	140
49. 庄子梦骷髅	142
50. 津人操舟	144

Chapter 5 Five Fifty Fables from Zhuangzi — 073

1. The Peng's Long Flight	075
2. Lady Li Weeps with Regret	075
3. Pounding on a Tub and Singing	075
4. Zhuangzhou Dreaming As a Butterfly	079
5. Learning How to walk in Handan	081
6. The Priest Overstepping the Duty of the Chef	081
7. Three at Dawn and Four at Dusk	083
8. The Penumbra Asking the Shadow	083
9. Cook Ding Carving Bulls	085
10. Sighing to the Sea	087
11. Boring for Chaos	087
12. The Unusable Tree	089
13. A Holy Man on the Faraway Mount Guye	091
14. A Mantis Trying to Stop a Chariot	093
15. Concentrated like a Wooden Cock	093
16. Dongshi Imitating Xishi	095
17. Mantis Catching the Cicada	097
18. Whirling Axe with Noise like Wind	097
19. Fish Watching on the Bridge of the Hao River	099
20. Obtaining a Valuable Pearl from the Black Dragon	099
21. Discarding the Trap after Catching the Fish	101
22. Yuanchu and Rotten Rat	103
23. The Fight Between the State of Man and Chu	103
24. An Enormous Fishhook with a Huge Line	105
25. No One Is Wise All the Times	107

26. Bian the Wheelwright Chiseling a Wheel	109
27. The Frog in the Well	109
28. Zhuangzi Borrowing Grain	111
29. Moving by Heavenly Mechanism	113
30. Licking Piles for Carriages	113
31. Differences Between Great and Small	115
32. A Salve to Prevent Chapped Hands	117
33. Xu You Resigning the Throne	119
34. A Huge Gourd of No Use	121
35. Qin Shi Mourning for Laozi	121
36. Zhili Shu Preserving Health	123
37. Wuzhi Striving to Learn	123
38. Zisang Contemplating Poverty	125
39. Tao of Robbers	127
40. A Man at Lvliang	127
41. Yunjiang Traveling to the East	129
42. Carving Wood into Ju	131
43. Duke Huan Seeing the Ghost	133
44. An Old Man Sticking Cicadas	135
45. All Wearing Confucian Dress in the State of Lu	137
46. Fetching Water to Water Fields	139
47. A White Horse Passing Through a Crevice	139
48. Tumors on the Elbow	141
49. Zhuangzi Dreaming of a Skull	143
50. A Ferryman Sailing	145

附录1：庄子思想导图	146
Appendix1: Mind Map of Zhuangzi's Thoughts	147
附录2：中国历史年代简表	148
Appendix2: A Brief Chronology of Chinese History	148
后记	151
Postscript	152

第一章

庄子其人

Chapter 1

An Introduction to Zhuangzi

一、宋国蒙人

庄子（约前369—前286年）的生平材料保存下来的很少。在《庄子·秋水》中记及楚威王用重礼聘请他为相，被他拒绝一事，司马迁在《史记》中为庄子所写的传也有这一记载，当是根据《庄子》采入。但《庄子》中有不少是寓言故事，楚王聘他为相的事是不是事实，很难确定。

禹田编著《〈史记〉故事中的大启发》中的庄子像

Image of Zhuangzi in *Englightment from Stories of "the Historical Records"* compiled by Yu Tian

最早记载庄子籍贯的是西汉史学家司马迁的《史记》。《史记·老庄申韩列传》云："庄子者，蒙人也，名周。"以后历代典籍也都以庄子为蒙人。今河南省商丘市梁园区李庄乡蒙墙寺村附近历史上有蒙泽，汉代曾在此设置蒙县。根据史料记载，结合考古发现，目前，大家比较一致地认为"蒙"地在河南省商丘古城北（偏东）25公里处，即今商丘市梁园区李庄乡蒙墙寺村。可以看出，庄子主要生活在以商丘为中心的古代河南、山东、安徽这一交界地带的黄河文明发源地，他的故事离不

I. From the State of Song

There are only a few of biographical materials of Zhuangzi (369-286 B.C.) recorded. According to "Autumn Floods" of *Zhuangzi*, it is said that King Wei of the Chu state invited him to be the prime minister with great courtesy but was refused by him. This can be found from Sima Qian's biography of Zhuangzi in *Historical Records* as well, which should be based on *Zhuangzi*. However, there are many fables in *Zhuangzi*. It is difficult to determine whether it is true that the king of the Chu state appointed him as prime minister.

The earliest record of Zhuangzi's native place is *Historical Records* by Sima Qian, a historian of the Western Han Dynasty. According to *Historical Records: Biographies of Laozi, Zhuangzi, Shenzi and Hanfeizi*, "Zhuangzi, whose name is Zhou, was born in the region of Meng, the state of Song." And then, all the scholars hold that Zhuangzi was from Meng in their classical records. There was Mengze in history near the village of Mengqiang Temple in Lizhuang Township, Liangyuan District, Shangqiu City, Henan Province, and Meng County was set up there in the Han Dynasty. According to both the historical records and

禹田编著《〈史记〉故事中的大启发》中的庄子像
Image of Zhuangzi in *Englightment from Stories of "the Historical Records"* compiled by Yu Tian

开这片钟灵毓秀的沃土。

庄子是宋国人。春秋战国时期的宋国,都于睢阳(今商丘市)。宋国的疆域在公元前481年灭掉北邻曹国后为最大,东面包括彭城(今江苏省徐州市)、宿(今安徽省宿州市),南面包括铚(今安徽省宿县西南)、酂(今河南省永城市西)、柘(今河南省柘城县),西部与魏国的宁邑(今河南省宁陵县)相邻,北部包括今山东省定陶,与鲁国的郓(今山东省郓城)相接。进入战国以后,形势便发生了很大变化,宋国在政治舞台上渐趋销声匿迹,辖地也逐渐减少,就在庄子去世的时候,宋国灭亡。

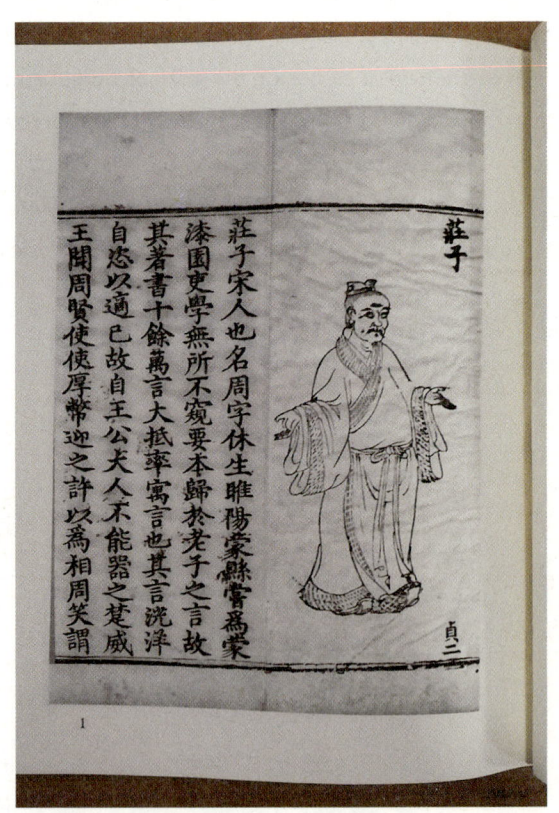

明正统年间《道藏》本《南华真经五卷》中的庄子像

Image of Zhuangzi in *Five Volumes of Nanhua Canon* in Zhengtong Period of the Ming Dynasty

archaeological findings, we mainly agree that "Meng" was located 25 kilometers north (by East) of Shangqiu ancient city, namely the present village of Mengqiang Temple in Lizhuang Township, Liangyuan District, Shangqiu City. Thus, it is widely acknowledged that Zhuangzi mainly lived in the border region of ancient Henan, Shandong and Anhui, with the center of Shangqiu city, where is the birthplace of the Yellow River civilization. So, his story is inseparable from this piece of land full of natural bestows.

Zhuangzi was born in the state of Song in the Spring and Autumn period and the period of Warring States. The state of Song was capitaled in Suiyang (now Shangqiu City).The territory of the state of Song was the largest after the perishment of Cao in 481 B.C., including Pengcheng (now Xuzhou City, Jiangsu Province) and Su (now Suzhou City, Anhui Province) in the east, Zhi (now southwest of Suzhou City, Anhui Province), Cuo (now west of Yongcheng City, Henan Province) and Zhe (now Zhecheng County, Henan Province) in the south, Ningyi (now Ningling County, Henan Province) of the state of Wei in the west, and Dingtao city, Shandong Province in the north connected with Yun (now

商丘市梁园区李庄乡蒙墙寺为商丘市重点文物保护单位
Mengqiang Temple of Lizhuang Township, Liangyuan District is the key cultural relics protection unit of Shangqiu City

庄子生活在宋国的衰亡时期,这种形势对庄子的思想产生了很大影响。由于庄子是当时著名的学者,楚威王曾派人到濮水请庄子做楚相,但被庄子拒绝。庄子曾到过梁国、齐国,见过梁惠王(前369—前319在位)和齐宣王(约前319—前301在位),还到过赵国和鲁国,可见其足迹遍布之广。

位于商丘市梁园区李庄乡蒙墙寺
Mengqiang Temple Located in Lizhuang Township, Liangyuan District, Shangqiu City

Yuncheng City, Shandong Province) of the state of Lu. Great changes had taken place in political situations in the beginning of the Warring States period, so the regime of the state of Song was decaying gradually. Just when Zhuangzi died, the state of Song perished.

Zhuangzi lived in the declining period of Song, which had a great influence on his thoughts. Because Zhuangzi was a famous scholar at that time, King Wei of Chu sent someone to the Pu River to invite Zhuangzi to be the Prime Minister of Chu, but Zhuangzi refused. Zhuangzi had been to Liang and Qi, where he met King Hui of Liang (369-319 BC) and King Xuan of Qi (319-301 BC). He had been to the state of Zhao and Lu, so his footprints were all over the country.

二、做官漆园吏

庄子出身贫寒，一生多数时间身居陋巷，靠编织草鞋、卖草鞋为生。司马迁《史记》记载庄子曾经为漆园吏，这也是庄子一生做过的最大的官职——管理漆园的小官。关于漆园吏，一说漆园为地名，庄子曾在此地做官。另一说是庄子曾在蒙邑为吏，主管漆树园。现在看来，不管是哪一种说法，漆园吏都是一个基层小官。由于庄子做过漆园吏，后世也常常以漆园吏代称庄子。据考证，这个"漆园"在今山东省东明县。

庄子对于做官并不感兴趣。他志向高洁，特立独行，始终保持着对富贵与权力的超脱，自甘淡泊，安贫乐道。有一次，梁惠王要见庄子，想提拔他做官。庄子便穿着打了补丁的破衣服，脚上穿着用草绳代替鞋带的破旧鞋子去见梁惠王。梁惠王见庄子这一身打扮，非常同情他，就说："听说你很有学问，没想到这么潦倒。"庄子听后，不以为然地说："衣服破了，鞋带掉了，谈不上潦倒，只是穷罢了。人有道德而不能施行，那才是潦倒。我之所以穷困，是因为我生在乱世，这是国家腐败造成的，我又有什么办法呢。"可见庄子并不是一个趋炎附势的人。

庄子家境很贫穷。一天，因家里实在揭不开锅了，便向监河侯借粮。监河侯说："行，我将要去封地收取赋税，你等着，一旦把税金全收上来，我借给您300金，好吗？"话说得很漂亮，但是没用，很显然是在搪塞庄子。庄子愤愤地说："我昨天在路上听见大呼救命的声音，一看，原来车辙里有一条快要干死的小鲫鱼，便问：'你叫什么呀？'小鲫鱼答道：'我是东海的大臣，您能给我一升水救救我吗？'我便说：'行。我将到南边去拜访吴越的大王，请他发西江的大水来迎接您，好吗？'小鲫鱼气愤地说：'我失去了经常相伴的水，以至落到这样的险境。我只要得到一升水就可活命，可您却说这样不着边际的话，还不如

II. Being an Official in Lacquer-yard

Zhuangzi was born and raised in a poor family. He lived in a shabby alley for most of his life and made a living by weaving and selling straw sandals. According to Sima Qian's *Historical Records*, Zhuangzi was once an official in lacquer-yard, which was the biggest official position Zhuangzi had ever held in his life — a small official in charge of the lacquer yard. As for the official of lacquer yard, it was said that lacquer yard was a place name, and Zhuangzi was an official in this place. And it was also said that Zhuangzi was an official in Mengyi, in charge of the lacquer yard. No matter what kind of view about the official, it was no doubt a grass-roots officer. So Zhuangzi was often called an official of lacquer yard by later generations. According to archaeological and textual research, this "lacquer yard" was located in present Dongming County, Shandong Province.

Zhuangzi was not interested in being an official. He was lofty minded and independent, and always kept aloof from wealth and power, willing to be indifferent and contented in poverty. Once, King Hui of Liang state wanted to see him, assigning him as an official. Zhuangzi went to see King Hui in his patched rags and worn-out shoes with straw ropes instead of shoelaces. Seeing his dress, King Hui sympathized with him and said, "I heard that you were very learned, but I didn't expect you to be so down and out." Zhuangzi retorted, "Although my clothes are ragged and shoelaces are off, it's not down and out, but just being poor. If a man is with morality but he can't carry it out, that's down and out. The reason of my poverty lies in that I was born in troubled times, which is caused by national corruption. That's none of my business." It can be drawn that Zhuangzi was not a man who went after the crowd.

Zhuangzi's family was too poor to serve a meal, so one day, he went to borrow grain from Marquis Jianhe. Jianhe said, "Well, wait, I'll go to the fiefdom to collect taxes. Once collected all the taxes, I'll lend you 300 gold, Ok?" That sounded reasonable but useless actually, which was obviously prevaricating Zhuangzi. Zhuangzi responded angrily, "I heard a cry for help on the road yesterday, taking a look, there's a carp in the rut that was about to die, and I asked, 'What's your name?' The little carp replied, 'I'm the minister of East Sea. Can you give me a liter of water to save me?' I said, 'No problem. I will go to the south to visit the

早些到干鱼市场上去找我吧。'"可以看出,庄子虽然幽默而有涵养,但并不是一个衣食无忧、生活富裕的人,他还要到处借粮,等米下锅。

根据庄子的兴趣来看,做官漆园吏,很可能不是庄子的主动选择,而是为了谋生,不得已才做出的选择。庄子穷了一生,却也快活自在地度过了一生。他看透了世俗的污浊,守住内心的自由自在,以自己的方式逍遥地生活在人世间。

king of the state of Wu and Yue, and ask him to send the flood of Xijiang River to save you, ok?' The little carp said angrily, 'I lost the water I used to accompany, and I fell into such a dangerous situation. As long as I get a liter of water, I can live, but you made such nonsense, so you might as well go to the dried fish market to find me earlier.'" It can be seen that although Zhuangzi was humorous and self-contained, he was not a wealthy man who had no worries about supporting a family. He had to borrow food everywhere for living.

According to Zhuangzi's interest, being an official in lacquer yard was probably not his active choice, but a choice he had to make in order to make a living. Zhuangzi was poor all his life, but he lived happily all his life. He saw through the filth of the world, kept his inner freedom, and lived freely in the mundane world in his own way.

三、钓于濮水

庄子不仅不愿意做像漆园吏这样职位低的小官,对于职位高的大官,庄子也不为所动。

古代,在今河南、山东交界处,有一条流经古菏泽区域的河流,叫濮水,是雷夏泽和巨野泽的水源之一。濮阳、濮州都从濮水得名。

有一次,庄子来到濮水边钓鱼。楚威王听说后,立即派两位大夫前去请庄子到楚国,想把楚国的内政交给庄子管理。正在钓鱼的庄子听到来意后,拿着钓竿,头也不回,两眼盯着水面说:"我听说楚国有一只神龟,死了已有3000年了,楚王用布帛覆盖着,用竹筐盛装着,藏在庙堂之上。这只神龟,是宁愿死后留下他的骨骸而显示其尊贵呢,还是宁愿活着,拖着尾巴在泥地里爬行呢?"两位大夫赶忙说:"它当然是宁愿活着拖着尾巴在泥地里爬行。"庄子说:"你们请走吧,我也打算拖着尾巴在泥地里爬行呢。"楚国的卿相之位,也没有能打动庄子。庄子不愿为外物所累,而是乐得自由自在,他不愿因做官而丧失个人的自由。

III. Fishing on the Pu River

Zhuangzi was not only unwilling to be a low ranking official like a lacquer yard one, but impervious to a high ranking official.

In the border region of nowadays Henan and Shandong in ancient times, there was a river flowing through the ancient Heze area called Pu River, which was one of the source waters for Xiaze and Juyeze (ze means marsh).Both the city of Puyang and Puzhou got their names from the Pu River.

Once, Zhuangzi came to the Pu River to fish. When King Wei of Chu state heard about it, he immediately sent two senior officials (Dafu) to invite Zhuangzi to the state of Chu to manage the internal affairs.When Zhuangzi, who was fishing, heard what they had come for, he took the fishing rod and did not turn his head back, "I heard that there was a tortoise in the state of Chu, which had been dead for 3000 years. The king of Chu covered it with cloth and put it in bamboo basket and hid it in the temple. Is this tortoise willing to show his dignity by leaving his bones after his death, or would he rather live and crawl in the mud with his tail?" The two officials made an instant answer, "He would rather live and crawl in the mud with his tail." Zhuangzi said, "Let me alone. I'm going to crawl in the mud, too." Zhuangzi was not moved by Chu's position as prime minister. He didn't want to lose his personal freedom for the external things such like being an official.

四、庄子与惠施

庄子的朋友不多,惠施是其中之一,而且是庄子最好的朋友。惠施也是宋国人,是当时著名的辩论家。在《庄子》中,经常能见到庄子与惠施辩论的场面,且常常都是针锋相对的,但这样的辩论并未影响二人的感情。

有一次,庄子与惠施在濠水的桥上观鱼。庄子见水里的鱼自由自在地游来游去,便向惠施感叹道:"你看这些鱼无忧无虑,自由自在,鱼也有鱼的快乐啊!"惠施一听,马上反驳庄子:"你不是鱼,怎么知道鱼的快乐呢?"庄子立刻反问一句:"你不是我,怎么知道我不知道鱼的快乐呢?"惠施说:"我不是你,当然不知道你。但你也不是鱼,一定也不知道鱼的快乐。"庄子又辩道:"你刚才说'你怎么知道鱼的快乐呢',就说明你已经知道我了。既然你知道我,我怎么不知道鱼呢?我就是在桥上知道了鱼的快乐啊!"庄子与惠施的辩论,既针锋相对,同时也有诡辩的成分。

还有一次,惠施做了梁国的相,庄子去拜访他。有人对惠施说,庄子此次到来,是想取代你的相位。惠施听了,便派人在城中搜了三天三夜。庄子听说后,便主动登门,还给惠施讲了一个故事:"你听说过凤凰吗?这种高贵的鸟从南海飞往北海,不是梧桐不歇脚,不是干净的果子不吃,不是甘甜的泉水不饮。有只鸱(鹞鹰)正在吃腐烂的老鼠,看到凤凰从头顶飞过,便护住腐鼠,冲着凤凰大叫,想吓走凤凰。惠施,你也想吓走我么?"通过这件事,惠施知道了庄子的志向远大。

惠施去世后,有一次庄子送葬,路过惠施的墓地。庄子回过头来对跟随的人说:"郢地有个人在自己的鼻尖上涂抹了白灰泥,像蚊蝇的翅膀那样大小、细薄,这个人让匠人用斧子削掉这个小白点。匠人挥动斧子,运斤成风,郢人听其挥削,鼻尖上的白泥完全除去而未伤着鼻子。

IV. Zhuangzi and Huishi

Zhuangzi had few friends, of whom Huishi is one and the best. Huishi was also a famous debater in the state of Song. It can be seen everywhere the scene of see-saw debating between Zhuangzi and Huishi in *Zhuangzi*, but that did not affect their close relations.

Once, Zhuangzi and Huishi were watching fish on the bridge of the Hao River. Seeing the fish swimming freely in the water, Zhuangzi sighed to Huishi, "Look, these fish are carefree, and they have their own happiness!" Huishi immediately refuted Zhuangzi, "You are not a fish; how do you know what constitutes the enjoyment of fish?" Zhuangzi retorted at once, "You are not me, how can you know that I don't know the happiness of fish?" Huishi said, "I'm not you, and of course I don't know you. But you are not a fish, so you must not know the happiness of fish." Zhuangzi argued again, "You just said, 'how do you know the happiness of fish'. That means you already know me. Since you know me, why don't I know fish? I know the happiness of fish on the bridge of the Hao River." The debate between Zhuangzi and Huishi was not only tit for tat, but also shew the sophism.

And at another time in history, Huishi became the Prime Minister of the state of Liang, and Zhuangzi went to visit him. Someone told Huishi that Zhuangzi was coming to scramble his position. After hearing this, Huishi sent people to search in the city for three days and three nights. Knowing that, Zhuangzi came to Huishi's house and told him a story, "Have you ever heard of the Yuanchu, the bird like Phoenix? This noble bird flies from the South Sea to the North Sea, and on its trip, it would not rest if it is not on Wutong tree, not eat if it is not clean fruit and not drink if it is not the sweet spring water. When a hawk is eating a rotten rat, he sees the phoenix flying over his head, so he protects the rotten rat and shouts at the phoenix to scare it away. Huishi, do you want to scare me away?" Through this event, Huishi knew Zhuangzi's ambition was great.

After Huishi died, Zhuangzi once passed Huishi's cemetery. He looked back and said to his followers, "There is a man in Ying who smeared lime mud on the tip of his nose, which is as thin as the wings of mosquitoes and flies. This man asks the craftsman to cut off the little white mud spot on his nose with an axe.

郢人站在那里若无其事，不失常态。宋元君知道了这件事，召见了匠人，说：'你为我也这么试试。'匠人说：'我确实曾经能够砍削掉鼻尖上的小白点。虽然如此，但是能够让我砍削的对象已经死去很久了。'自从惠施离开了人世，我没有可以匹敌的对手了！我也没有能够与之论辩的人了！"

"运斤成风"意为手法熟练，技艺高超，而匠人能够运斤成风，需要胆大的郢人配合。惠子是庄子的朋友，也是辩论对手，惠子死后，庄子失去了对手和知音。可见，庄子与惠施私交很好。同样，通过惠施与庄子的交往，也能看出庄子宁可选择贫困、自由自在地生活，也不愿意做自己不喜欢的事情。

When the craftsman waves his axe with noise like wind, the white mud spot is completely removed without hurting his nose. Ying man stands there as usual as if nothing has happened. When Duke Yuan of Song knew this, he summoned the craftsman and said, 'Try it for me'. The craftsman said, 'I really used to be able to cut off the white spot on the tip of nose. However, the man who trusts me and lets me chop has been dead for a long time.' Since Huishi died, there is no close opponent whom I can argue with!"

"Waving Axe with Noise like Wind" refers to the supreme skill of the craftsman who may rely on the trust and cooperation of the man from Ying. Huishi was Zhuangzi's friend and opponent. After Huish died, Zhuangzi lost his opponent and confidant. We now understand that Zhuangzi and Huishi had a good personal relationship. Similarly, through the communication between Huishi and Zhuangzi, we can see that Zhuangzi would rather live in poverty and freedom than do things he does not like.

五、庄子之墓

庄子能坦然地对待死亡，把个人的生死看成自然现象，同时反对厚葬。庄子快要死的时候，弟子们打算用很多的东西为他陪葬。庄子说："我把天地作为棺椁，把日月作为美玉，把星辰作为珠宝，万物都来陪葬。难道这么多的葬物还不算齐备吗？还有什么比这更好的呢？"弟子们说："我们担心乌鸦和老鹰会啄食先生的遗体。"庄子说："其实放在地面会被乌鸦和老鹰吃掉，深埋于地下会被蚂蚁吃掉，夺过乌鸦和老鹰的食物交给蚂蚁吃，怎么能如此偏心呢？"庄子视天地为棺椁，将死看成回归自然，这在当时是非常难能可贵的。

民权县老颜集乡的庄子陵园
Cemetery of Zhuangzi in Laoyanji Township, Minquan County

庄子死后，弟子们到底是怎样处理庄子遗体的，现在无从知晓了。但后世很多地方都出现了庄子墓，如河南省民权县老颜集乡唐庄村的庄

V. The Tomb of Zhuangzi

Zhuangzi can treat death calmly, regard personal life and death as a natural phenomenon, and oppose the elaborate funeral. When Zhuangzi was about to die, his disciples planned to bury him with a lot of funeral things. Zhuangzi said, "I take heaven and earth as coffin, sun and moon as jade, stars as jewelry, and all things are buried with me. Aren't so many funeral objects enough? What could be better?" The disciples said, "We are afraid that crows and eagles will peck at your body." Zhuangzi replied, "In fact, above ground, I will be eaten by crows and eagles. Below ground, I will be the food of ants. How can you be so partial to prefer the later one?" Zhuangzi regarded heaven and earth as coffins and death as returning to nature, which was very valuable at that time.

位于民权县老颜集乡的庄子墓
Tomb of Zhuangzi located in Laoyanji Township, Minquan County

After the death of Zhuangzi, it was impossible to know how the disciples dealt with his body. However, there were many places where Zhuangzi's tomb appeared in later generations, such as Tangzhuang Village, Laoyanji Township Minquan County, Zhuangying Village, Liugu Township, Huaxian County

子墓,滑县留古乡庄营村的庄子墓,山东省东明县菜园集乡庄寨村的庄子墓,安徽省凤阳县临淮镇濠水之畔的庄子墓,等等。可见,庄子这个名人,最终的归宿地与他的出生地一样,都受到了后人的重视,以商丘为中心的古代河南、山东、安徽这一交界地带,都是庄子的故乡故土。

安徽省蒙城县庄子祠
Memorial Temple of Zhuangzi in Mengcheng County of Anhui Province

(the above two places are in Henan Province); Zhuangzhai Village, Caiyuanji Township, Dongming County, Shandong Province; the riverside of the Hao River, Linhuai Town, Fengyang County, Anhui Province, and so on. It can be seen that Zhuangzi's ultimate destination, like his birthplace, has been valued by later generations. The Ancient areas Henan, Shandong and Anhui, with Shangqiu as the center, are the hometown of Zhuangzi.

第二章
庄子的思想学说

Chapter 2

The Theory and Thought of Zhuangzi

一、宇宙观

庄子认为"宇宙"是无始无终、无边无垠的,并将宇宙的根源归结为"道"。在庄子看来,人的感性和理性所能感知和推测的事物,都不可避免地带有相对性与有限性,生死、贵贱、大小、是非、善恶、美丑、荣辱、得失等,都是人们心中的成见,是人们被自己有限的认知能力所遮蔽而导致的。

庄子认识到了事物之间存在着普遍的差异,而差异不是绝对的,而是相对的。庄子认为这种相对性来自于人类自身的种种局限,因为世间万物本没有差别,所谓差别,都是人们站在主观立场上而得出的相对结论。他同时又肯定虽然事物存在着相对性,但对立的双方又互为对方存在的条件,是不可以完全消除的。他说:"知东西之相反而不可以相无。"(《秋水》)这种相对主义思想,主宰了庄子对于自然、社会、人生等各个领域的认识与理解,但也必然将他带入不确定的混乱之中,于是庄子虚构了一个空虚的绝对——"道",来消除这种相对性带来的不确定性。他认为不论世间万物有如何的差别,一旦站到更高的"道"的角度去审视,这种种差别都将消失不见。他还认为,虽然事物之间没有特定的标准来彼此衡量,但只要将万物都归结到一个统一的本原,即"道"之中,就没有任何的差别了,"道"在这里成了一个绝对的标尺。

庄子认为,"道"有情有信,无为无形;可传而不可受,可得而不可见。"有情有信",说明道是客观存在的;"无为无形",则道又是没有意志、没有形体的虚无存在;"可传而不可受,可得而不可见",是说道是超乎感知,无法掌控的。此外,他还认为道是万物产生的本原,先天地生而不为久,长于上古而不为老,是超脱了时空限制的,是绝对的。

Ⅰ. Cosmology

Zhuangzi holds that the universe is endless and boundless, and he attributes the origin of the universe to "Tao". He retains that people's sensibility and rationality which can be perceived and inferred are inevitably relative and limited. Life and death, eminent and humble, big and small, right and wrong, good and evil, beautiful and ugly, honor and disgrace, gain and loss, and so on, all of are prejudice rooted in people's hearts, caused by people's limited cognitive ability.

Zhuangzi realizes that there are universal differences between things, and the differences are not absolute, but relative. Zhuangzi believes that this relativity comes from the limitation of human beings, because there is no difference in all things in the world. The so-called difference is the relative conclusion that people draw from the subjective position. At the same time, he also affirms that although there is relativity in things, the opposite sides are the conditions for each other's existence, which cannot be completely eliminated. He said, "We should know that east and west are opposite but mutually indispensable."("The Floods of Autumn")This relativism dominated Zhuangzi's understanding of nature, society, life and other fields, but it also brought him into the confusion of uncertainty. So Zhuangzi makes up an empty absolute "Tao" to eliminate the uncertainty brought by this relativism. He believes that no matter how many differences between things in the world, once we look at them from a higher angle of "Tao", these differences will disappear. He also believes that although there is no specific standard between things to measure each other, but as long as all things are attributed to a unified origin, namely "Tao", there will be no difference, thus, "Tao" has become an absolute ruler here.

Zhuangzi maintains that "Tao" has its reality and its signs but with no action and form; it can be transmitted but not taught, obtained but not seen. "A reality which has its substance" means that Tao indeed exists; "it has its own source and root" means that Tao exists in itself; "it begets the heaven and the earth" means that Tao gives birth to heaven and earth and everything in the world; "Inaction and formless" shows that Tao is an vacant existence without will and form; "transmitted but not taught, obtained but not seen" shows that "Tao" is beyond perception and control. In addition, he also believes that Tao is the origin of all

庄子肯定"道"是先于天地而存在的，但也肯定当天地万物生成之后，道便存在于天地万物之中。因此，当东郭子向他询问道存在于何处时，他便说在"蝼蚁""稊稗""瓦甓""屎溺"之中，并告诉东郭子，道的本质并不是存在于某一个特定的事物中，而是普遍存在于万事万物之中的，因此越是取喻于卑下的事物，就越是能说明大道无处不在的道理。

正由于"道"是生养天地万物的根源，且无处不在，故人与天地万物从根本上是同根同源且地位平等的，因此庄子说："天地与我并生，而万物与我为一。"(《齐物论》)这种"天人合一"的思想，成了中国古代哲学的基本精神。这种精神从对自然的思索出发，更重视人与自然的和谐统一，与以社会伦理规范为出发点、致力于道德修养实践的儒家精神一起，构成了中国古代哲学完整而稳定的结构。

(宋)林希逸《庄子鬳斋口义》，宋刻本
Carving copy of *Yanzhai's Understanding of Zhuangzi* by Lin Xiyi (Song Dynasty)

things, and before heaven and earth existed, it is firmly there from ancient times, which is beyond the time and space limit, so it is absolute.

Zhuangzi affirms that "Tao" exists before heaven and earth, but he also affirms that when all things in heaven and earth come into being, Tao exists in them. Therefore, when Dongguozi asked him where it existed, Zhuangzi answered, it was in the "ant, "panic grass", "tiles and shards" and "piss and shit". Furthermore, he told Dongguozi that the essence of Tao did not exist in any specific thing, but in universal things. Therefore, the more humble things were taken for example, the more eloquent it was to illuminate the universal existence of Tao.

It is because "Tao" is the root of all things in heaven and earth, and it is everywhere. Therefore, mankind and all things in heaven and earth have the same root, the same origin and equal status, so Zhuangzi said, "heaven and earth are born at the same time I am, and the ten thousand things are one with me."("Making All Things Equal")This ideology of "the unity of man and nature" has become the basic spirit of ancient Chinese philosophy. This Taoist spirit emphasizes the harmonious unity between man and nature by taking the nature as its source; while the Confucian spirit focuses on devoting to the practice of moral cultivation. Both of them constitute the basic structure of ancient Chinese philosophy.

二、认识论

在认识论方面，庄子意识到了人类认识领域内的一些矛盾，这些矛盾来源于人类认识的种种局限——感官经验的局限，个人思维的局限，时间、空间的局限，等等，这些局限使人类在认识上很难达到完全的统一，而往往表现出某种相对性。这种相对性常常是令人困惑和不安的，因此，人们一直在寻找超越这种相对性的绝对的"真知"。可在庄子看来，由于认识有局限而被认识的对象无限，人类获得"真知"显然是一件十分困难的事情："吾生也有涯，而知也无涯，以有涯随无涯，殆已！"（《养生主》）可见，庄子认为人的认识能力极其有限，而认识的对象却是无穷无尽的，以有限的能力去探求无限的知识，显然是十分困难的。庄子认为"真知"是有的，但并非人人皆有，"知天""知人"还只是"知之盛"，仍有所待，只有为"真人"所掌握的时候才能变为一种"真知"而上达于"道"。很显然，庄子认为"真人"之所以能掌握"真知"，最主要的一个原因在于他突破了人的感官局限，具有了超乎常人的思维能力，因而能认识到"知之所不知"这种超越人们感官体验的事物。

当然，并非人人都能成为"真人"，掌握"真知"，但人们可以努力超越自身狭隘的认识，扩大自身的认识能力与范畴。当获得足够丰富的感官经验时，则可能将这些感官经验上升到新的层次，从而得到新的更高层次的知识，所以，庄子认为庖丁之所以能将解牛之技运用得神乎其神，就在于他能将感官经验上升到理性经验，从而使其解牛的技艺远远超越了其他人。

庄子不仅肯定了"真知"的存在，而且肯定了"真知"是可以"闻"，可以"体"，可以"守"的。他经常提到的"闻道""体道""守道"，就是获得"真知"的几种途径。而如何"闻道""体

II. Epistemology

In terms of epistemology, Zhuangzi is aware of some contradictions in the field of human cognition. These contradictions come from various limitations of human cognition, for example, the sensory experience, personal thinking, time and space, etc. These limitations make it difficult for human beings to achieve complete unity in cognition, but often show some relativity. This relativity is often confusing and disturbing, so people have been looking for absolute "true knowledge" beyond this relativity. However, Zhuangzi maintains that it is very difficult for human beings to acquire "true knowledge" because our cognition is limited but the universal things are limitless. "I have a limit in my life, and there is no limit in my knowledge. If you use what is limited to pursue what has no limit, you will be in danger." ("Essentials for Keeping a Good Health"). Zhuangzi realizes that people's cognitive ability is extremely limited, but the object of knowledge is endless, so it is obviously very hard to explore infinite knowledge with limited ability. Zhuangzi holds that "true knowledge" exists, but not everyone can achieve it. "Knowing heaven" and "knowing man" are just "the perfection of knowledge", which still needs to be developed. Only when they are understood and mastered by the "true man" can they become a kind of "true knowledge" to achieve "Tao". Obviously, Zhuangzi thinks that the main reason why the "true man" could master "true knowledge" is that he has broken through the limitations of human senses and has extraordinary thinking ability, so he can realize the thing that "use the knowledge of what one knows to help out the knowledge of what one doesn't know".

Of course, not everyone can become a "true man" and achieve "true knowledge", but people can transcend their own limited cognition and expand their own cognitive ability and scope. When one has accumulated enough sensory experiences, which may rise on a new level, one may get the new knowledge of this level. Therefore, Zhuangzi thought that Cook Ding's miraculous skill of cutting bulls lied in that he could raise the sensory experience to rational experience and made his skill far surpass others.

Zhuangzi not only affirms the existence of "true knowledge", but also affirms that "true knowledge" can be "heard", "embodied", and "held". He often refers to

道""守道",庄子提出了"以明""见独""坐忘"的方法。所谓"以明",实际上就是消除是非偏见,以空明若镜的心灵来观照万物。而"见独"与"坐忘",其实是一种精神修养方式,由此方式达到内心的虚静忘我,最终进入精神上一片混沌的状态。在这个过程中,人以一种神秘的直觉大彻大悟,并获得感官经验所不能提供的"真知"。

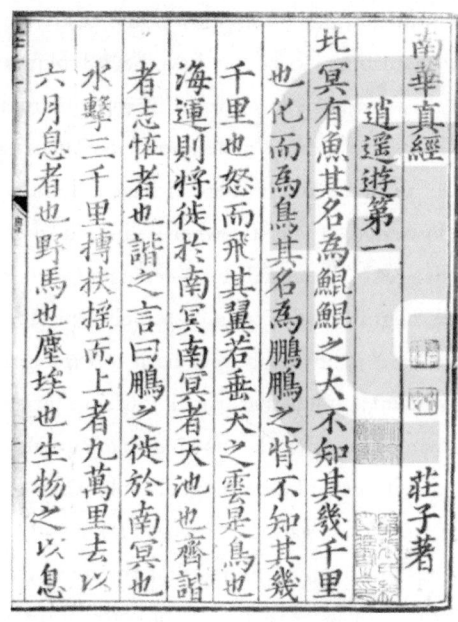

《南华真经》明刊本

Printing Version of *Nanhua Canon* in the Ming Dynasty

several ways to obtain "true knowledge", including "hearing Tao", "embodying Tao" and "holding Tao". He further puts forward the methods of "using clarity", "discerning the independent Tao" and "sitting and forgetting" so as to achieve the above three ways to obtain "true knowledge". The so-called "using clarity" is actually to eliminate the prejudice of right and wrong, and to observe all things with an empty and clear mind. And "discerning the independent Tao" and "sitting and forgetting" are actually ways of spiritual cultivation, from which we can achieve inner emptiness and selflessness, and finally enter into a chaotic state of no difference in spirit. In this process, man comes to a thorough understanding with a mysterious intuition, and obtains the "true knowledge" that sensory experience cannot provide.

三、人生观

庄子的人生观首先立足于解决人生困境，与其他先秦诸子将眼光落于短暂而有限的现实社会不同，庄子一开始就企图为人类寻找一个不仅摆脱现实社会困境，而且摆脱最终生命困境的途径。因此，庄子一方面要求鄙弃人间的世俗道德、功名利禄，以达到远祸全身、逍遥自适的境界；另一方面要求齐同生死，不悦生亦不恶死，从而超越死生，达到真正自由的目的。

庄子认为要达到最大的精神自由，首先要认识到人同自然界其他事物一样，都经历着由生至死的过程。庄子意识到，人之生死犹如昼夜交替，是人力无法改变的，因此，悦生恶死都是不必要的。面对生死最好的态度就是"安之若命"，因为"天地负载着我的形体，让我活着的时候劳苦，使我衰老闲逸，使我死后得到休息"（《大宗师》），自然赋予人形体，就是要让人生时勤劳，老时安逸，死时休息，这是一个自然而必然的过程，所以应当"善吾生"亦"善吾死"，将生死都看成一件美事。如果连生死都可"安之若命"，那么世俗的情感则更能以一种平静的态度去面对。庄子认为各种情感都会伤身，人一旦被生死、好恶等束缚，便会累如倒悬，相反，如果能齐同生死，忘却情感，便能不为外物所伤。

庄子人生观的最高境界体现在那些具有理想人格的至人、真人、神人、圣人身上。这些理想形象的最大特点就是能超然世外，无往而不逍遥。他们一方面能超脱死生，另一方面能超脱世俗道德与情感，同时还具有一套养生之法。他们具备能够超乎常人，具有一些令人惊讶的能力，能够"不吃五谷杂粮，吸着大风，饮着露水，驾着云气，乘着飞龙，遨游于四海之外"（《逍遥游》），或是"巨大的山泽燃烧起来也不能让他感到炎热，黄河、汉水冻结起来也不能让他感到寒冷，迅雷震

Ⅲ. View of Life

Zhuangzi's view of life is based on solving the dilemma of life. Different from other pre-Qin scholars who focus on the short and limited normal life society, Zhuangzi tries to find a way for human beings to get rid of not only the dilemma of real society, but also the ultimate dilemma of life. Therefore, on the one hand, Zhuangzi advocates to despise worldly morality, fame and wealth, so as to achieve the state of being far away from the disaster, keep the body in good health and enjoy oneself in absolute freedom; On the other hand, he asks us to take equal attitude toward the personal life and death, neither be happy with life nor disgusted with death, so as to surpass life and death and achieve the goal of absolute freedom.

Zhuangzi believes that to achieve the absolute spiritual freedom, one must first recognize that human beings, like other things in nature, are experiencing the process from life to death. Zhuangzi realizes that human life and death, like the alternation of day and night, cannot be changed by a human being, so it is unnecessary to love life and hate death. The best attitude to life and death is "to be content with it as with fate", because "there is the heaven and earth I find the support of my body in, which make me toil when I live, get old in leisure, and rest after I die" ("Great Master"). Nature endows human body that is to make human beings hard-working when living, getting old leisurely, and rest after die. This is a natural and inevitable process, so it should be "it's good for being alive", and "it's good if I died", thus to regard both life and death as a beautiful thing. If life and death can be taken by us who are "to be content with them as with fate", and then secular emotions can be faced with a calm attitude. According to Zhuangzi, all kinds of emotions will hurt us. Once we are bound by life and death, likes and dislikes, we will be as tired as hanging upside down. Oppositely, if we can take equal attitude toward life and death, and forget emotions, we will not be hurt by any external things .

The highest realm of Zhuangzi's view of life is embodied in those perfect men, true men, holy men and sages with ideal personality. The most important characteristic of these ideal images is that they can be detached from the outside world. On the one hand, they can get rid of life and death, and on the other hand,

撼着高山，狂风掀起海浪也不能让他受惊害怕"（《齐物论》）。这是庄子眼中处世的最高境界，但也只能是一种理想的追求与向往，人总是要生活在某个特定的历史与社会之中的，因此，更现实的问题还在于如何避免外物对于本性的摧残，而达到"自救"。由此，庄子提出了"避世"和"游世"的办法，以求在乱世之中保全自我。庄子认为"无用"是自我保全的途径之一，栎社树、商丘之木因"不材"而得以长寿，牛之白额头者、猪之亢鼻者、人有痔病者因不可祭神而得以保全自身，形体不全的人以外形残疾，身生痼疾而得以"终其天年"，因此，庄子感叹有用不如无用好。

避世的直接目的还是为了保全自我，相比于儒家对现实的积极肯定、参与和改造，这种与现实保持距离的做法无疑是消极的，但它又是建立在对自身精神世界的自信与认真之上的。这种精神上的洁癖，要求远离世俗世界的污浊，从而保全精神世界的洁净与高贵。

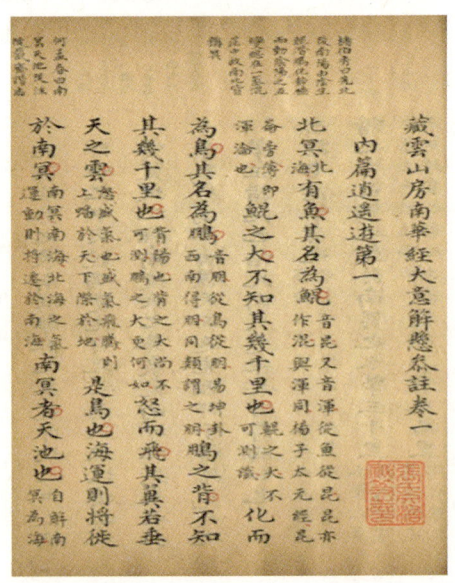

普林斯顿大学东亚图书馆藏清代《藏云山房南华经大意解悬参注》

Annotation of Nanhua Canon by Cangyunshanfang holding by East Asian Library of Princeton University

they can get rid of secular morality and emotion, also at the same time, they have a set of health preserving methods. They have some amazing abilities which make them surpass ordinary men, such as "not eating the grains, but sucking the wind, drinking the dew, riding on the cloud, harnessing the flying dragon and roaming beyond the four seas" ("Wandering in Absolute Freedom"), or "great lakes might be boiling about him, and he would not feel the heat; the Yellow River and the Han River might be frozen up, and he would not feel the cold; the hurrying thunderbolts might split the mountains, and the wind may shake the ocean, without being able to make him afraid." ("Making All Things Equal") This is the highest realm in Zhuangzi's eyes, but it can only be an ideal pursuit and yearning. We always have to live in a specific history and society, so the more realistic problem is how to avoid the destruction of true nature by external things and achieve "self-help". Therefore, Zhuangzi puts forward the methods of "retiring from the world" and "wandering in the world" in order to preserve himself in the troubled times. Zhuangzi maintains that "being unusable" is one of the ways to self-preservation. The serrate oak and Shangqiu wood live a long life because they are unusable. Bulls with white foreheads, pigs with turned-up snouts, men with piles can save them because they can't be offered as sacrifice to the river god, the crippled men with incomplete body can "live out the years heaven gave". Therefore, Zhuangzi believes that it's better to be unusable than usable.

Compared with Confucianism's positive affirmation, participation and reform of reality, the idea of escaping from the world and keeping a distance from reality for preserving oneself is undoubtedly negative. But this is also based on self-confidence and seriousness in one's own spiritual world. This kind of spiritual cleanliness requires keeping away from the filth of the secular world, so as to keep the spiritual world clean and noble.

四、政治观

庄子的政治观来源于他对所处时代的体验。战国中晚期,政治上表现出前所未有的动荡与不安。战争给人民的生活带来了痛苦,权术也将人们的精神推向了险恶境地,《庄子》中多次写到的战争、暴君、权臣等,都是这种社会状况的直接体现。庄子认为当时所存在的政治制度、道德法度是完全多余的,道德仁义不过是诸侯用来窃国的工具,仪则法度也不过是统治者的欺诈行为。如果硬要以道德法度来约束、欺骗百姓,则必然造成"子有杀父,臣有杀君"的严重后果。

庄子认为,天地万物的发展都应循其自然之道,人与社会也应如此,所以他提出了废弃君臣之分、复归原始的返璞归真思想,并为人们勾画了一个无等级君臣,废除仁义道德,消除欲望机心,使人与人之间和谐共处的理想社会。

IV. Political Views

Zhuangzi's political views originate from his experience of his time. In the middle and late Warring States period, there was unprecedented turbulence and uneasiness in politics. The war brought pain to the people's life, and political tactics also pushed people's spirit to an unstable depressed condition. Zhuangzi quite often wrote about the war, tyrant, and powerful minister and so on, which are the direct embodiment of social situation at that time. According to Zhuangzi, the political system and moral laws of that time were totally superfluous. Moral benevolence and righteousness were just tools used by vassals to steal the power of the country, and the ritual laws were just the fraud of the rulers. If we insist on using moral laws to restrain and deceive the people, it will inevitably lead to the serious consequences of "sons killing their fathers, ministers killing their rulers".

Zhuangzi thinks that the development of all things in the world should follow the way of nature, so as man and society. So he puts forward the idea of abandoning the distinction between monarch and minister and returning to the original, thus to draw a blueprint of the ideal society where there is no difference of classes, no pursing of humanity and morality, and people can live in harmony with each other.

五、美学观与文艺观

庄子的美学观来源于他的哲学观，因此，他眼中的美并不是纯粹的自然美或艺术美，而是与"道"合一的境界美。人一旦做到"天地与我并生，而万物与我为一"（《齐物论》）、"独与天地精神往来"（《天下》），就能从天地万物中体验到一种人与自然合一的愉悦感，这在庄子看来才是美的极致。因此，庄子的美学观从一开始就有两个指向，一个指向外部形体的自然之美，另一个指向内部的无为素朴之美。

庄子肯定外部形体之美，并且认为这种美来自"天地"之间。他曾对大自然的美景进行过细致描摹，诸如大海仙山、日月星辰、飞禽走兽、雷电风雨等，构成了一幅幅大自然的壮阔景象。但庄子认为："天地有大美而不言。"（《知北游》）美来自"天地"之间，并非仅仅由表象而做出的判断。"天地有大美"的原因在于它能顺应大道，自然无为。所以，庄子笔下的至人、真人、神人，往往具有极美的外形，其前提也是能顺应大道，无为虚静。庄子不但认为只有这种虚静恬淡、素朴无为的精神状态才能体验到美，同时也认为这种虚静恬淡、素朴无为的精神本身就具有一种美，这种美甚至还远远超越于形体的美。所以，"德有所长而形有所忘"（《德充符》），即使外形丑陋，只要具有精神之美，就能得到人们的钦慕。

反之，对天然本性的摧残就是对美的破坏，使其失去了原本天然的美。如，他认为，"百年之木"，枝叶繁茂，一旦被砍去，即使做成尊贵的"牺尊"，涂上青黄的花纹，但失去了其天然本性，也是不美的。再如，怡然自得的海鸟，一旦被"御而觞之于庙"，即使是"奏《九韶》以为乐，具太牢以为膳"，但失去了其自然生存的环境，也无美可言，最终"三日而死"（《至乐》）。

庄子将自然素朴、不加雕琢虚饰的美称为"真"，他认为："真，

V. Aesthetic and Literary Views

Zhuangzi's aesthetic view comes from his philosophical view, so the beauty in his eyes is not pure natural one or artistic one, but the beauty of merging with "Tao". Once men realise "heaven, earth and myself come into existence at the same time; all things are one with self."("Making All Things Equal") and "immerse into the spirit of heaven and earth alone" ("The World"), they can experience a kind of pleasure of merging men and nature from all things in the world, which is the ultimate beauty in Zhuangzi's view. Therefore, Zhuangzi's aesthetic view has two tendencies from the very beginning: one turns to the natural beauty of external form, and the other turns to the simple beauty of internal inaction.

Zhuangzi affirms the beauty of external form, and believes that this beauty comes from the "heaven and earth". He once made a detailed description of the beautiful scenery of nature, such as the sea and celestial mountains, sun, moon and stars, fowls and beasts , thunder, wind and rain and so on. However, Zhuangzi holds that "heaven and earth have their great beauties but do not speak of them".

("Zhi Traveling North") Beauty cannot be judged by superficial presentation but from "heaven and earth". The reason why "heaven and earth have great beauty" lies in that it can conform to Tao, natural and doing nothing. Therefore, perfect men, true men and holy men in Zhuangzi's works often have extremely beautiful forms, which rely on their conformant to Tao, achieving emptiness and stillness by doing nothing. Zhuangzi not only holds that only in the simple, inactive, empty and still state of spirit, can we experience beauty, but also thinks that this spirit itself is a kind of beauty which far surpasses the beauty of the body. Therefore, "if virtue is preeminent, the physical form will be forgotten" ("Sign of Complete Virtue"). Even if the appearance is ugly, as long as obtaining the beauty of spirit, one can get admiration from others.

Instead, the destruction of the nature is to destroy the natural beauty. For example, as long as "the hundred-year-old tree " is hacked up to make noble bowls for the sacrificial wine, with blue and yellow patterns on them, it has lost its original nature and beauty. Another example is the happy seabird. Once it alighted in the suburbs of the Lu capital, the marquis of Lu escorted it to the ancestral temple, where he entertained it, "performing the Nine Shao music for

就是精诚到了极致。如果不纯真，不诚实，就不能感动他人。……内心纯真，就表现于神色，这就是真，所以宝贵。……礼，是世俗之人所制定的；真，是天赋的，自然而不可改变的。所以圣人效法天然，看重纯真，不受世俗约束。"（《渔父》）这种"法天贵真"的美学观点不仅表现在反对人工雕琢、追求事物天然本真，而且表现在推崇纯真率性、自由不羁的人格上。

庄子的美学观又极大地影响了他的文艺观。由于认为"美"在于"真"，在于自然无为，因此，文艺创作应当以还原本真为目的，在自然无为的态度下进行，这就要求摒弃一切功利目的，使文艺创作成为一种自然而然、合乎本性的行为。他以赌博作比，认为如果用便宜的瓦器作赌注，就会心无顾忌而赌得很好；若以较贵重的带钩做赌注时，就会心怀忌惮而赌不好；要是拿黄金做赌注，就会心慌意乱，彻底昏聩。庄子借这则故事说明只有忘掉利害得失，超越功利欲望，才能全神贯注、闲暇自得地运用技艺。

同时，由于庄子认为最高层次的美是超越形体之外的精神美，所以表现美的文艺创作也应该基于一种内在的精神体验，只有忘却外物，与天地精神往来，做到与"道"相通，才能创作出好的艺术作品。庄子认为，列御寇射箭的技艺虽高，可是一旦"登高山，履危石，临百仞之渊"（《田子方》），便发挥不出来了，就是由于还未达到物我两忘的境界。庄子还将艺术的产生归结为一种神秘的直觉领悟，即"心斋""坐忘"，这是一种靠直觉和灵感获得创作源泉的方式。但是庄子并非认为艺术创作的源泉是凭空而来的，或是一种虚无的存在，相反，他认为艺术创作只可能建立在大量现实经验的基础之上，如《达生》中的粘蝉老人，其高超的粘蝉技艺，是经过"累丸二而不坠""累三而不坠""累五而不坠"这几个艰苦的训练过程才达到的；心不旁骛，用心专一，聚精会神于一处，心中想的都是蝉翼，自然粘蝉技艺高超。《养生主》中庖丁解牛，也经过了最初的"所见无非牛者"；三年之后，

it and presenting it with the meat of the Tailao sacrifice to feast on , " the seabird has lost its natural living environment and beauty, and finally, it "died in three days" ("Supreme Happiness").

Zhuangzi calls the natural and simple beauty as "truth". He said, "Truth is the absolute of purity and sincerity. If you are not pure and honest, you can't move others…This truth resides within and performs expressions , and this is why we count it so valuable.…Propriety is made by secular men; truth is innate, natural and unchangeable. Therefore the sages take their law from nature, and prize their (proper) truth, without submitting to the restrictions of custom."("The Fisherman")Zhuangzi's aesthetic view of "patterning oneself on Heaven and prizing the truth" is not only reflected in his opposition to artificial carving and polishing, but in his pursuit of the natural truth, but also in his praising the free personality beyond worldly restraints.

His aesthetics greatly influenced his view of literature and art as well. Because of the view that "beauty" lies in "truth" and in natural inaction, literary and artistic creation should be carried out in the attitude of natural inaction with the purpose of restoring the truth, which requires abandoning all utilitarian purposes, so as to make literary and artistic creation an original natural behavior. He takes gambling as an example, and he argues that if one bets with a piece of cheap earthenware, he will put forth all his skill in winning without scruple; if the prize is a buckle of brass, he may shoot timorously; if he bets with gold, he may lose his wit as if he were blind. Zhuangzi shows us only by forgetting the gain and loss of profit and passing the desire of utility can we concentrate on using skills freely.

In the meanwhile, Zhuangzi thinks that the artistic works of expressing beauty should also be based on an internal spiritual experience which is the supreme beauty beyond physical form. Only by forgetting the external things, immersing into the spirit of heaven and earth, and connecting with "Tao", can good works of art be created. Zhuangzi holds that although Lie Yukou is skillful in archery, once he "climbs a high mountain, treads over the tottering rocks, and faces the brink of eight-hundred-foot chasm" ("Tian Zifang"), he cannot put forth his skill. That is because he hasn't reached the state of forgetting both things and oneself. Zhuangzi also attributes the emergence of art to a mysterious intuitive understanding that is, "fasting of the mind" and "sitting and forgetting", which

"未尝见全牛也";方今之时,"以神遇,而不以目视,官知止而神欲行"这几个过程才达到的。同时,庄子又主张在获得技巧之后最终要将技巧忘却,如工倕之所以能成为巧匠是因为他不但不依据规矩,也不受心思的指使,完全凭手指自然而然地进行创造。

当然,庄子并不主张进行人为的艺术创造,在他看来,艺术创造是内在精神体验的外在表现,而内在精神所依据的"道"本身却是"不当名"的,因为"道不可闻,闻而非也;道不可见,见而非也;道不可言,言而非也"(《知北游》)。这就是人们常说的"可意会而不可言传",事物最深奥的"妙理"是无法用语言来表达的,只有"求之于言意之表","入乎无言无意之域"(郭象《秋水注》),才能掌握。毕竟"道"作为一个抽象的概念,本来就无法具体描摹,一旦描摹出来,它也就不再是原本意义上的"道"了。由此,庄子认为语言、形式所能表达的只是事物粗糙的外表,用语言文字所写的书籍,也不过是一堆糟粕。

另外,庄子认为一定要进行艺术创造的话,也应该是"意在笔先"。他在《田子方》中说,宋元君请画工画图,画工们都到了,恭恭敬敬地"揖礼之后而立,有的用口水润笔,有的调色",只有一个画工迟迟而来,"安闲自在,慢慢进来,行礼之后并不站在一边,而是回到了客馆"。宋元君派人去查探,发现他赤身裸体,分开双腿坐在那里,宋元君于是认为他才是真正会画图的人。宋元君做出这种判断不是没有道理的,因为,此画工不但能赤身裸体,去除形体上的负担,而且心理上能神闲气定,超然物外,作画时也就必然能够凝神于笔端,达到精神与外物合而为一的状态。

are ways to obtain the source of creation by intuition and inspiration. That does not mean that Zhuangzi thinks that the source of artistic creation comes from nothing, or an existence of emptiness, but based on a large number of practical experiences. For example according to "Full Understanding of Life", the old man's excellent skill of sticking cicada is mastered through three hard training processes, including "balancing two balls on top of each other without falling", "putting two on the top of the pole without falling" and "adding five is the same". That is due to his concentration on one place and on one thing, that is the cicada wings. Cook Ding's carving the bull in *Essentials for Keeping a Good Health* also went through three stages: the initial state of "nothing but bull"; the second stage after three years, when he no longer saw the bull as a whole but in parts"; and the last stage of "getting at it by spirit but not by looking with eyes. Perception and understanding have come to a stop, and spirit moves where it wants" has been achieved. Zhuangzi, in the meanwhile, also advocates that after acquiring skills, one should finally forget them. For example, the reason why Chui the artisan became a craftsman is that he does not follow the rules, nor instructed by his mind, but he creates by his fingers naturally.

Of course, Zhuangzi here does not advocate artificial artistic creation. He believes that the artistic creation is the external manifestation of inner spiritual experience, which is based on Tao which should not be given a name, because "Tao cannot be heard, and if heard, it is not the Tao; Tao cannot be seen, and if seen, it is not the Tao; Tao cannot be spoken of, and if spoken of, it is not the Tao ("Zhi Traveling North").This is the common saying that "the meaning can be understood but can't be explained in words". The most profound "wonderful Tao" of things can't be expressed in words. Only by free wandering of "seeking from the words and meaning" and "entering into the realm of no words and no meaning" (Guo Xiang's *Commentary on "The Floods of Autumn"*), can we master it. After all, "Tao", as an abstract concept, cannot be described concretely. Once described, it will no longer be "Tao" in its original sense. Therefore, Zhuangzi summarizes that language and form can only express the rough appearance of things, and the books written in language are just a pile of dross.

In addition, working of artistic creation must be carried out by "meaning first" but not started with the pen. According to "Tian Zifang", Duke Yuan of

唐庄村庄子墓前的亭子下有清乾隆五十四年重修庄周墓石碑
Stele of Rebuilding Zhuangzi's tomb in the 54th year of Qianlong's Period of the Qing Dynasty in the pavilion, in front of Zhuangzi's tomb, Tangzhuang Village

Song once summoned the painters to have a map drawn. They all came and "stood after bowing, moistened their brushes with saliva, and toned their colors" except one who came late, "with an air of indifference, and did not hurry forward. After saluting, he didn't stand aside, but returned to the inn". Duke Yuan sent a man to see him, and there he was, almost naked, with his upper garment off, and sitting cross-legged. So Duke Yuan thought that he was the true artist who really knew how to draw. It's not unreasonable for Duke Yuan of Song to make such a judgment, because the painter can not only be naked and remove the burden on the body, but also be calm, relaxed, and keep aloofness over the external things on mind. When he paints, he must be able to concentrate on painting and achieve the state of merging spirit with the external things as one.

第三章

庄子的文学艺术特色

Chapter 3

The Literary and Artistic Characteristics of

Zhuangzi

一、寓言、重言、卮言

寓言、重言、卮言的运用，是《庄子》一书最重要的艺术特色。

《庄子》"寓言十九"。寓言是《庄子》一书中最重要的表现手法。《史记·老庄申韩列传》说："其著书十余万言，大抵率寓言也。"《庄子》全书大小寓言共计200多个，其短者只有十几个字，其长者有的达到1000多字。有些篇目全部由寓言排比而成，有些篇目干脆通篇就是一个寓言。庄子的寓言，是在"天下一片污浊，不能严肃地与他们交谈"（《天下》）的情况下诞生的。北冥之鱼可以千变万化，鸟类向高空盘旋飞翔扶摇而上九万里；藐姑射山神人可以不食五谷、吸风饮露；任公子可以用五十头牛为饵来垂钓；空骷髅也可以与人娓娓交谈。总之，一切有形的与无形的，无一不可化为故事，来表达庄子的哲学。在《庄子》中，这种寓言的成分占得最多。但是，《庄子》中的寓言又非常与众不同。先秦其他诸子，如孟子、韩非子等人亦可谓善用寓言，但孟子多采用民间传说故事来加强自己的论辩，韩非子多利用历史传说与典故以佐证自己的说理，而《庄子》的寓言却大多"皆空语无事实"(司马迁语)，而且庄子对于这些"无事实"之语，还往往辅以细致生动的描写，使之不仅有情节，还有对话，有形象，有情感。正是这些天马行空、看似虚妄的想象、虚构与描写，使《庄子》一书在哲学的成分以外，带上了奇幻斑斓的文学色彩。

"重言"则是借重古代圣哲或是当时名人的话，来休止天下的争辩之言。但是庄子的实际用意，并不是为了推崇圣哲与名人。虽然庄子有"齐物论"之心，却也不得不站出来说话，因此只好退而求其次，借着偶像说自己的话，以避免纠缠于世俗的是非之争。因此，庄子在创作"重言"时，时而借重黄帝，时而借重老子，时而又求助孔子，当然，他们虽然披着圣贤的外衣，却在说庄子的话。所以，虚构圣哲与名人的

I. Fables, Quoted and Random Talks

The most important artistic feature of *Zhuangzi* is the use of fables, quoted and random talks.

"The fable takes up nine-tenths" of *Zhuangzi*, which is the most important technique of expression in the book. According to *Historical Records: Biographies of Laozi, Zhuangzi, Shenzi and Hanfeizi*, "Zhuangzi wrote more than 100,000 words, most of which are fables." There are more than 200 fables in *Zhuangzi*, some of which are only in dozen words, and some longer ones contain more than one thousand words. Some chapters are all made up of fables, while others are complete fables. Zhuangzi's fable was born under the condition that "people of the social world were lost to the pleasures of the material wealth and could not be argued with or reasoned with" ("The World")The fish of the North Sea can make endless transformation, when it changed into a bird, it could hover high in the sky and beat the whirlwind and rise ninety thousand Li. There is a holy man living on faraway Mount Guye. He doesn't eat the five grains but sucks the wind and drinks the dew. A young nobleman from the state of Ren can use 50 cattles as bait to fish; empty skull can also talk with men. All of these wise sayings which have form and even the ones that do not can be transformed into stories to express Zhuangzi's philosophy. This kind of fable accounts for the most part in *Zhuangzi* but they are quite different from the common fables. Other pre-Qin scholars such as Mencius and Han Feizi are also good at using fables. However, Mencius uses folklore to strengthen his argument; Han Feizi uses historical legends and allusions to prove his reasoning. However, most of the fables in *Zhuangzi* are empty words without facts (Sima Qian's criticism). Furthermore, Zhuangzi often supplements these words with detailed and vivid description, either about the plot or the dialogue, the image or the emotion. It is these illusory imagination, fiction and description that make *Zhuangzi* take on the fantastic and colorful literary color beyond the philosophical elements.

"Quoted talks" refer to quoting the words of ancient sages or celebrities at that time to stop the augmentation of the world. But Zhuangzi's real intention is not to praise sages and celebrities. Although Zhuangzi maintains the idea of "making all things equal", he has to ask help from the idols to advocate his idea

言论在庄子笔下是司空见惯的事，甚至历史上的人物不够用了，他还会另造出许多"乌有先生"来，让他们谈道说法，互相辩论。"重言"的运用，使《庄子》一书带有了一种亦庄亦谐的色彩，并将庄子的思想表达得倍加灵动新奇。

"卮言"在《庄子》中游衍不定。卮，古代的酒器。庄子以"卮言"命名，是想表明自己所说的话如酒器里的酒，"卮满则倾，卮空则仰，空满任物，倾仰随人"，都是无心之言，所以称为"卮言"。正因为是无心之言，时倾时仰，因此"卮言"大多是些不着边际的议论，想到哪儿说到哪儿。在处于乱世之中的庄子看来，百家争鸣，各执一端，尤其儒、墨二家，他们妄论是非、善恶、贵贱、高下，完全是由于自私用智，为成见所固蔽，所以庄子想以"卮言"的形式，跳出是非争辩的圈子，避开自我成见的干扰，期合于天然的端倪，而顺应大道的运行。

《庄子》一书中，寓言、重言、卮言是"三位一体"，浑不可分的，它们互相辅助，互相映衬，构成了《庄子》"汪洋恣肆"的语言艺术特色。庄子正是以其杰出的天才、超人的想象、浪漫的感情，借助"三言"打破言与意的隔膜，创造出极具浪漫主义感染力的优美文字，成为中国文学中不可逾越的高峰。

so as to avoid entanglement in the secular dispute between right and wrong. Therefore, when Zhuangzi wrote "quoted talks", he sometimes borrowed from Yellow Emperor, Laozi and Confucius. Of course, they were speaking for Zhuangzi although they were wearing the coat of sages. Therefore, it is common for Zhuangzi to make up the opinions of sages and celebrities. Even if there are not enough historical figures, he will create many "Mr. Nothing" to let them talk about Tao and argue with each other. The application of "quoted talks" makes *Zhuangzi* full of solemn and humorous characteristics, and the expression of Zhuangzi's thoughts are more flexible, vivid and novel.

"Random talks" in *Zhuangzi* are indefinite. "Zhi" was originally an ancient wine vessel, which was borrowed by Zhuangzi as "random talks" to show that his words are like the wine in the wine vessel, "when it is full, we drink forward; when it is empty, we lean backward. Empty or full, that is the wine's usual quality; forward or backward, that depends on the drinker's action. Both of them are at random." That is like the random talk, which may be spoken unintentionally. It is just because they are unintentional words, which are inclined forward or backward, so the "random talks" are mainly irrelevant discussion spoken freely and randomly. Zhuangzi comments on a hundred schools of thoughts who contend with each other, especially the Confucians and the Mohists are blinded by the preconceived ideas to argue about right and wrong, good and evil, eminent and humble, superior and inferior, so, he wants to use "random talks" to break the confinement of the arguing on wrong and right and avoid the interference of self-prejudice, hoping to conform to the nature and the law of Tao.

Fables, quoted and random talks are closely related and complemented with each other, which can be taken as a trinity, and composed of the artistic features of *Zhuangzi's* "unrestrained and romantic" language style. With his outstanding genius, superhuman imagination and romantic feelings, Zhuangzi connected words with meaning with the help of "three talks" (fables, quoted and random talks) and created beautiful words with great romantic appeal, which has become an insurmountable peak in Chinese literature.

二、庄子散文的艺术特色

庄子散文在先秦诸子中最具特色。其散文的独到之处，便是它跳出了先秦语录体散文与论辩体散文的束缚，不仅以说理为目的，还创造了一种优美飘逸、恢恑憰怪的文学风格，使其散文的文学性甚至超越了哲理性。

这种文学性，首先表现在创造了一大批鲜明的形象。这些形象的创造，并不限于人物，而且还借助寓言为载体，超越了常人的认知与想象，延伸至自然界一切有形无形的事物，甚至存在于人们观念中的精神事物。这些形象或美或丑，或真或假，或庄或谐，或逍遥或狭隘，令人目不暇接。在人物方面，庄子创造了一批极有特色的至丑之人，《大宗师》中描写子舆得病，以至于背偻腰曲，五脏脉管突起于背脊，脸缩于肚脐，肩高于头顶，身体完全扭曲变形，却不但不以之为丑，反而"心闲无事"，摇晃着走到井边，欣赏自己变形的躯体，实在令人匪夷所思。《德充符》中，庄子更是集中塑造了一批身残形丑之人，这些人不是缺胳膊少腿，便是形貌丑陋变形，甚至长着碗大的瘤，可谓丑之极致，但庄子却对他们赞叹不已，不仅让孔子在他们面前恭敬有加，还让他们与老聃谈道论法。当然，庄子也并非专门制造一些丑陋的形象来哗众取宠，《逍遥游》中描写藐姑射之山的神人，"皮肤洁白如冰雪，安静柔弱又似处女；不吃五谷杂粮，吸着大风，饮着露水，驾着云气，乘着飞龙，遨游于四海之外"，完全是形德之美的极致。《大宗师》中也描写了真人，"心思专一，外貌平静，额头高凸宽大而质朴。面容看上去像秋天一样明净，像春天一样温暖。他的喜怒哀乐就像四季更替一样，顺应事务变化却无人知道其定则"，其美简直能令天地变色。除了这些或美或丑的虚构形象，庄子笔下还有像孔子、颜回这样的儒家人物，文惠君、卫灵公、惠施这样的执政者，匠石、轮扁、庖丁、梓庆这

II. The Artistic Features of Proses in *Zhuangzi*

Zhuangzi's prose is unique in characteristic among the writings of pre-Qin scholars. The unique feature of his prose lies in its reasoning purpose, graceful, humorous and grotesque style, which breaks away from the bondage of the popular ana and argument in the pre-Qin period, and thus makes his prose more literary than philosophical.

This kind of literariness is first manifested in the creation of a large number of distinctive images. These images are not confined to human characters, but extending to both formless things and physical forms, and even the spiritual things only in people's mind. All of the images are embodied in the fables which are beyond ordinary people's cognition and imagination. These dazzling images are beautiful or ugly, true or false, solemn or humorous, carefree or narrow-minded. In the aspect of characters, Zhuangzi created a group of extremely ugly people. In the "Great and Venerable Master", it is described that Ziyu is so sick that his back sticks up like a hunchback, his vital organs are on the top of his back, his chin is hidden in his navel, and the shoulders up above his head, and his body is completely distorted. However, Ziyu does not regard him as ugly, instead, he "has nothing to do with his mind", and is wandering to the well to appreciate his distorted body. That is really amazing. In "Signs of Complete Virtue", Zhuangzi focuses on creating a group of disabled and ugly people who are either short of arms and legs, or ugly and deformed, even with bowl-sized tumors, which can be called the ultimate ugliness. However, Zhuangzi praises them, which not only makes Confucius show great respect to them, but also makes them talk with Laozi. Of course, Zhuangzi does not just create some ugly images to attract the attention of the public. He also describes some ultimate beautiful characters. For example in "Wandering in Absolute Freedom", Zhuangzi depicts a holy man living on faraway Mount Guye, "with skin like ice or snow and gentle and shy like a virgin. The holy man does not eat the grains, but sucks the wind, drinks the dew, rides on the cloud, harnesses the flying dragon and roams beyond the four seas." That is the ultimate beauty of both form and virtue. In "Great and Venerable Master", Zhuangzi also describes the true man, who is "concentrated and calm in appearance, with high convex forehead, broad and simple. His face

样的普通职业者。不仅人类，甚至自然界的万事万物都可以为庄子所用，成为其寓言中的主人公，栎树可以托梦给匠石，讲述无用以全身的道理；髑髅可以与庄子同寝，讨论死生之间的际遇；甚至连影子及影子外的虚影也能交谈，不能不让人赞叹庄子的奇思妙想。

漫无涯际的想象与广阔无垠的视野，又使庄子散文能够超越时空的局限，呈现出宏大雄奇的气魄与汪洋恣肆的浪漫主义色彩。在庄子笔下，北冥的巨鲲有几千里之大，一朝化而为鹏，其翼便如垂天之云，能够水击三千里，扶摇而上九万里。任公子垂钓，要大钩巨缁，以五十头牛为饵，蹲于会稽山上，投竿东海，一年过去，大鱼吞饵，顿时白浪如山，海水震荡，声如鬼神，震惊千里，鱼之大，可令浙江以东、苍梧以北之人均得饱食。《齐物论》中的至人，"巨大的山泽燃烧起来也不能让他感到炎热，黄河、汉水冻结起来也不能让他感到寒冷，迅雷震撼着高山，狂风掀起海浪也不能让他受惊害怕。……驾着云气，乘着日月，而遨游于四海之外"。这些气势宏大的描写，可谓道尽了"大"的玄妙，不能不唤起人们对逍遥的无限遐想。

庄子又不时以大手笔来曲尽"小"之情状，《则阳》中讲"蜗牛左角有个国家，名曰触氏；蜗牛右角有个国家，名曰蛮氏"，蜗角之国，已经小而又小，然而就在如此小的地盘上，触、蛮二氏却还能"时相与争地而战，伏尸数万，逐北旬有五日而后返"，实在令人惊心动魄、难以置信。然而，这又正是战国时期动乱社会的真实反映。庄子也正是以这种夸张之语，来嘲讽目光浅陋、厮杀无止的诸侯。而将这种雄奇的夸张发展到极致是在庄子将死之时，"弟子们想厚葬他。庄子说：'我把天地作为棺椁，把日月作为美玉，把星辰作为珠宝，万物都来陪葬。难道这么多的葬物还不算齐备吗？还有什么比这更好的呢？'"（《列御寇》)意思是只有在精神上冲出渺小的个体，将短暂生命融入宇宙万物之间，方能有此不惧死生的气魄。试看先秦诸子，除了庄子，又有谁能有这种精神上的无限张力，这种穿越时空、超越死生的旷达情怀呢？

looks as clear as autumn and warm as spring. His joys and sorrows are like the turning of seasons which adapts to the natural changes, but no one knows the Tao". That is the extreme of beauty. In addition to these fictional images of beauty or ugliness, there are also Confucians such as Confucius and Yan Hui, and rulers like Lord Wenhui, Duke Ling of Wei and Hui Shi; ordinary men such as Jiangshi the Carpenter, Lunbian the Wheelwright, Cook Ding and Ziqing the Carpenter. Not only human beings, but also everything in nature can be the protagonist in Zhuangzi's fables. Serrate oak may appear in Jiangshi the Carpenter's dream to tell him the Tao of self-preservation by "being unusable". The skull can sleep with Zhuangzi to discuss the life and death. Even the penumbra can talk with the shadow which makes us admire Zhuangzi's fantastic ideas.

The boundless imagination and the vast vision make Zhuangzi's prose transcend the limitation of time and space, and present a magnificent and romantic color. In *Zhuangzi*, the giant Kun (a fish) of the North Sea is thousands of Li in size. Once it was transformed into a Peng (a bird), it can hover high in the sky and beat the whirlwind and soaringly rise ninety thousand li. When a young nobleman from the state of Ren was fishing, he had to take a fish hook with a huge line, and use 50 cattles as bait. He would squat on Kuaiji Mountain and cast a pole into the East China Sea. A year later, the huge fish swallowed the bait. Suddenly, the white cap of the sea was as high as a mountain, and the sound of the sea was like ghosts and gods. This huge fish could make everyone in the east of Zhejiang and the north of Mount Cangwu have a good meal. In "Making All Things Equal", there are perfect men who have some amazing abilities. "Great lakes might be boiling about him, and he would not feel their heat; the freezing of the Yellow River and Han River can't make him feel cold; the hurrying thunderbolts which can split the mountains and the wind shake the ocean, can't make him afraid....He rides on the cloud, harnesses the sun and the moon, and roams beyond the four seas." These magnificent descriptions can manifest the subtlest mysteries fully, and cannot help arousing people's infinite reverie about the absolute freedom.

Sometimes, Zhuangzi uses a magnificent and detailed description to explain the situation of "small". In "Zeyang", it is said that "on top of the left horn of a snail, there is a state whose ruler is called Chu, and on top of its right horn there is

庄子散文的形象和气势，还通过生动贴切的比喻和细致传神的描写来表现。例如，《养生主》篇以薪喻形，以火喻神，薪有尽而火无穷，正如形体总有枯槁之时，但精神只要加以保养便能不穷不尽，强调了养生者当在于养神而非养形。又如，《在宥》篇以"焦火"喻其躁，"凝冰"喻其坚，"俯仰四海"喻其速，"渊静县天"喻其动静各殊，皆用来比喻人心之不可撄。庄子在运用比喻时，还往往善于使用连绵作比的博喻，造成如层峰起伏般的奇妙效果，如《天运》"孔子西游于卫"一段，接连使用"古今非水陆""周鲁非舟车""桔槔俯仰""柤梨橘柚可口""猿狙衣周公之服""西施病心而矉其里"六个比喻，作六层转换，生动地说明"礼义法度"必须"应时而变"的道理。

细致传神的描写也是庄子散文艺术魅力的来源之一，它使庄子散文不仅有故事，而且情节生动有趣；不仅有人物，而且人物栩栩如生。情节、语言、动作、神态、心理活动等，各方面惟妙惟肖。《盗跖》是一个典型代表，"孔子见盗跖"的过程，就是一篇完整的小说，情节跌宕起伏，引人入胜：被人称为"圣之和也"的柳下惠与"杀人放火"的盗跖成了亲兄弟，相隔百年的孔子与柳下惠居然也成了好友；孔子一意孤行，不听劝阻，欲说服盗跖改邪归正，不料却遭盗跖痛斥，落荒而逃，路遇柳下惠，发出"我就是那种没病而自己非要针灸的人""差一点儿被老虎吃了的人"的感叹。整个故事大起大落，变幻莫测，生动地刻画了盗跖与孔子的形象。特别是孔子失败遭斥、狼狈而逃时的形象描写："孔子再次行礼，慌忙退出，出门上车，手上的马缰绳多次掉在地上。两眼茫然，什么也看不见；面色像死灰一样苍白。扶着车轼，低着头，大气也不敢出。"短短几句神态与动作描写，孔子失魂落魄、狼狈而逃的模样便跃然纸上。

庄子散文的文学成就，还表现在其语言特色上。庄子的语言往往如行云流水，飘逸优美，宛转跌宕，同时又节奏鲜明，音调和谐，具有诗

a state whose ruler is called Man. Even in such a small territory, "these two states often fight for territory and go into wars with tens of thousands of corpses left on the ground. The victors have to chase for fifteen days before they return home". It's really breathtaking and unbelievable. However, this is the true reflection of the turbulent society in the Warring States period. It is with this exaggeration that Zhuangzi mocks the shortsightedness and endless fighting of princes. Such an exaggeration has been developed to the peak in depicting Zhuangzi's death. When Zhuangzi was about to die, the disciples wanted to bury him. Zhuangzi said, "I take heaven and earth as coffin, sun and moon as jade, stars as jewelry, and all things are buried with me. Aren't so many funeral objects enough? What could be better?" ("Lie Yukou")That means only when we get beyond the small individuals in spirit, and integrate the limit life into the universe, can we have the courage of facing death and life. In addition to Zhuangzi, who could have such unlimited spirit, such broad-minded feelings of crossing time and space and transcending life and death among all the pre-Qin scholars?

The image and momentum of Zhuangzi's prose are also expressed through vivid and appropriate metaphor and detailed description. For example, in the chapter of "Essentials for Keeping Good Health", wood is used to describe the form and fire the spirit. The wood may be used up but fire is endless, just as the body must be withered, but the spirit can be endless as long as it is maintained. It emphasizes that people of health preserving should cultivate the spirit rather than the body. Another example is that in "Let be and Let Alone", it will become as hot as the fire when the mind is restless, or as cold as the ice when it is firm. The change of the mind is so swift that just between lifting and lowering the head, it has twice swept over the world. When it is at rest, it is deep and still, when in movement, it is far and long as the heaven, all of which is to show that people's mind cannot be meddled with. Zhuangzi is also good at using metaphors continuously and in layers of depth to create wonderful effects. For example, in the passage of "Confucius' journey to the west in the state of Wei" in "Movements of Heaven", he successively uses six metaphors: "Are the past and present not like the water and the land", " Are the states of Zhou and Lu not like a boat and a cart", "Turning back when they have reached the limit", "The haw, the pear, the orange, and the citron are all pleasing to people's mouth", "If you dress a monkey in the

位于商丘市民权县庄子镇的庄子井

Zhuangzi Well, located in Zhuangzi Town, Minquan County, Shangqiu City

一般的艺术效果。如《齐物论》中对风的描写，极写了风之情态，从各种各样的孔穴，写到各种各样的风声，从小风到大风，再到众窍俱寂，树影摇曳。既有赋的铺陈，又有诗的节奏，读来仿佛令人身临其境，领略了一番自然的变幻莫测。在行文构思上，庄子散文的文字散而有结，开阖无端，首尾不落俗套，转接无露痕迹，令读者忽如置身群峰之间，忽如脚踏平原之上，忽如登临万仞之巅，一览无遗，忽如误入十里迷津，惝恍迷离。

robes of the Duke of Zhou, it may bite and tear at them", and "The beauty Xishi, troubled with heartburn, frowned at her neighbors". All the above six metaphors are used successively to explain the idea vividly that "rites, righteousness and legalities" must "change according to the time".

Detailed and vivid description is also one of the sources of artistic charm of Zhuangzi's prose, which is with great stories and interesting plots, lifelike characters, whose language, action, manner, and psychological activities, etc. are vivid. The description of Confucius seeing the robber in "Robber Zhi" is a representative of the prose which is a complete novel with ups and downs and fascinating plots: Liu Xiahui, who is known as "Holy Harmony", has shared the true brotherhood with the robber Zhi, who is "killing and setting fire". Confucius and Liu Xiahui, who are separated by a hundred years, have become good friends; Confucius went his own way to persuade robber Zhi to mend his ways. Unexpectedly, he was denounced by Zhi and ran away. When he met Liu Xiahui on the way, he sighed that "I'm the kind of person who didn't have any disease but had to prick acupuncture himself" and that "I was almost eaten by a tiger". The whole story is full of ups and downs and unpredictable plots, vividly depicting the images of robber Zhi and Confucius. In particular, the description of Confucius' image of being criticized and in a panic run: "Confucius saluted again and hurried out; outside the gate, he climbed into his carriage and fumbled many times in attempt to grasp the reins. His eyes were blank and nothing to see; His face was as pale as ashes. Holding the bar of the carriage, and lowering his head, he did not dare even to gasp." In just a few words of describing the facial expression and action, Confucius's appearance of being out of his wits and running away in a panic stands vividly on the paper.

The literary achievement of Zhuangzi's prose is also reflected in its linguistic features. Zhuangzi's language is often like flowing water, elegant and beautiful, and full of ups and downs. At the same time, it has distinct rhythm and harmonious tone, which has poetic artistic effect. For example, the description of wind in "Making All Things Equal" describes the modality of wind in its summit, from all kinds of holes to all kinds of wind sounds, from small wind to strong wind, and then to the silence of all orifices and the swaying of tree shadows. There are not only the elaborations of Fu (an intricate literary genre), but also the

与先秦其他诸子散文一样,《庄子》还是以说理为目的的散文,只是庄子以其令人惊叹的天才,不自觉地在文学性上超越了哲理性。正如闻一多所说:"庄子是一位哲学家,然而侵入了文学的圣域。"(《古典新义·庄子》)正由于此,庄子能把枯燥艰涩的理论表达得浑然流畅,含而不露。庄子汪洋恣肆的生花妙笔根本上还是来源于其深邃难测的哲理,读《庄子》不仅要欣赏其艺术魅力,也应当领略其哲学风采。

rhythm of poetry. It seems that people are personally on the scene and appreciate the natural changes. In the style of writing, Zhuangzi's words seem scattered but have the ending, and both the beginning and end are unconventional, without the trace of transition, which makes the readers feel as if they are among the peaks, and suddenly, as if they are stepping on the plain, or sometimes as if they are climbing on the top of the mountain to enjoy the scenery with one glance, and still sometimes as if they are straying into a lost with blank eyes.

Like other pre-Qin prose, *Zhuangzi* is still a prose aiming at reasoning, but with his amazing genius, he unconsciously transcends philosophy in literariness. As Wen Yiduo said, "Zhuangzi is a philosopher, but he has invaded the holy land of literature."(*New Explanation of the Classics: Zhuangzi*)It is for this reason that Zhuangzi can express the seemingly boring and difficult theory smoothly in subtle and indirect way. Zhuangzi's unrestrained and brilliant writing is rooted in his profound and unpredictable philosophy. To read *Zhuangzi*, we should not only appreciate its artistic charm, but also make sense of its philosophy.

第四章

庄子的历史地位及影响

Chapter 4 The Literary and Artistic Characteristics of Zhuangzi

庄子在文学上的影响很大，自贾谊、司马迁以来，无一不受他的熏陶与影响，闻一多说："中国人的文化上永远留着庄子的烙印。"(《古典新义·庄子》)

第一，在先秦诸子中，庄子可谓最善于将寓言作为一种文学形式加以自觉运用的。在他笔下，寓言不仅仅是说理的辅助工具，也具有了几近独立的地位。在中国文学的发展过程中，它直接影响了文人的寓言创作，如唐代韩愈的《马说》《龙说》《送穷文》，柳宗元的《三戒》《种树郭橐驼传》，明代刘基的《郁离子》等，使寓言逐步脱离了论说文、史传文而独立成体。更为重要的是，先秦寓言起着上继神话，下启小说的作用。《庄子》中关于对浑沌、黄帝、广成子等人物形象的刻画，都采用了神话题材，其变幻莫测的想象与夸张也与古代神话的风格相似。但它又发展了神话的简单形式，其寓言有故事情节，有时甚至是复杂的故事情节，有人物形象，有对话，有细节，直接启发了后代小说的产生。《庄子》中许多寓言记述或者虚构了鬼怪异事，是魏晋以后志怪小说的鼻祖之一。《庄子》中鼓盆而歌的寓言，在冯梦龙《警世通言》中被发挥成《庄子休鼓盆成大道》。庄周梦蝶、髑髅见梦等寓言，也被后人演绎为《三勘蝴蝶梦》《大劈棺》等戏剧，鲁迅《故事新编》中的《起死》也本于此。至于后代诗、词、曲、赋中熔铸其寓言为题材的，更是俯拾皆是，数不胜数。

第二，庄子"独与天地精神往来"(《天下》)的浪漫主义风格也给中国文学带来了深刻的影响。其极端热情的文字，漫无涯际的想象，缤纷瑰丽的辞藻，天马行空的文思，使其成为中国浪漫主义文学的源头，影响到包括咏怀诗、玄言诗、游仙文学、山水文学、田园文学、志怪文学等在内的一大批文学形式。唐代李白深受庄子"开浩荡之奇言"的浪漫主义风格影响，其诗歌、散文感情炽烈，想象丰富，气势磅礴，狂放不羁，成为庄子之后中国浪漫主义文学的又一个高峰。宋代苏轼也深得庄子浪漫主义真谛，他说："吾昔有见于中，口未能言。今见《庄

The influence of Zhuangzi on Chinese literature is so great that since Jia Yi and Sima Qian, many have been influenced by him. Wen Yiduo said, "The Chinese culture always bears the brand of Zhuangzi." (*New Explanation of the Classics: Zhuangzi*)

First of all, among the pre-Qin scholars, Zhuangzi is the best at consciously using fables as a literary form. In his works, the fable is not only an auxiliary tool of reasoning, but also an independent literary form. In the development of Chinese literature, it directly affected the creation of fables, such as Han Yu's *On Horse*, *On Dragon*, and *Farewell Poverty*, Liu Zongyuan's *Quit in Three Aspects*, *The Biography of Guo Tuotuo, a Tree-Planter* in the Tang Dynasty, and Liu Ji's *Yulizi* in the Ming Dynasty, which gradually separated fables from argumentation and historical biography, thus made it an independent literary form. More importantly, the pre-Qin fables play the role of bridge by following the myth and enlightening the novel. *Zhuangzi*, in the depiction of the characters such as Chaos, Yellow Emperor, and Guangchengzi, adopts mythological themes, and their unpredictable imagination and exaggeration are similar to the style of ancient mythology. But it also develops the simple form of mythology into fables with complicated plots, characters, dialogues and details, which directly inspire the creation of novels of later generations. There are many fables in *Zhuangzi* containing strange things about ghosts, which are one of the originators of mystery novels after Wei and Jin dynasties. The fable of singing while playing drums is developed into " Story of Zhuangzi' Cultivation for Tao" in Feng Menglong's *Stories to Warn Men* .The fables of Zhuangzhou's dream as a butterfly, and skull's dream have also been interpreted by later generations as such dramas as "Three Explorations of Butterfly Dream" and "The Resurrection", which are also the origin of "Revive" in Lu Xun's *Old Tales Retold Stories*. As for the poems, Ci, Qu and Fu of later generations, there are many themes of fables.

Secondly, Zhuangzi's romantic style of "immerse into the spirit of heaven and earth alone" ("The World") also has a profound impact on Chinese literature. Its extremely enthusiastic writing, boundless imagination, colorful and magnificent rhetoric, and unrestrained train of literary thought make *Zhuangzi* the source of Chinese Romantic literature, and affect a large number of literary forms, including poems of nostalgia, metaphysical poetry, literature of immortals,

子》，得吾心矣。"(苏辙《亡兄子瞻端明墓志铭》)表明其自然旷达、卓尔不群的人格，其《赤壁赋》及清风阁、凌虚台、墨宝堂、超然台诸记，思想语言亦无不出于《庄子》，而其文章所谓"如行云流水""如万斛泉源，不择地而出"的风格，亦与《庄子》相近，其词更是得庄子之风，开创"豪放词"一派。

第三，庄子散文中的美学思想对中国文学、艺术都产生了深远的影响。庄子认为，"天地有大美而不言"(《知北游》)，"美"存在于"天地"之间，为自然所有。这一思想可谓直接孕育了中国山水诗、田园诗、游记等文学的萌芽，并促其发展。中国的绘画、书法也无一不受其影响，山水画以其得天地之美而成为中国画的最主要类型，书法则受其"大美"的美学情调和浪漫主义风格的影响，产生了行云流水、挥斥八极的草书，典型的如张旭、怀素等人的书法。庄子还独开"以丑为美"的美学先河，他不追求形体的完美，但更追求精神的完美。庄子以形体的丑陋来突出精神之美的美学取向，也成了后世文学家和艺术家们的又一灵感源泉，文学家以"丑石""病梅"等有缺憾的事物来表达自己的精神追求，画家们则多以形象怪异丑陋的人物来表达内心不屈不挠的精神力量。此外，庄子主张得意忘言、言约旨远、意在言外的创作准则，直接影响了刘勰"情在词外"、钟嵘"文有尽而意有余"、司空图"象外之象，景外之景"、王国维"境界说"等文艺理论和文学批评思想。

第四，庄子蔑视权势利禄、追求独立自由人格和逍遥自适的精神，使中国文人在儒家的"修身、齐家、治国、平天下"之外，有了另一种生命追求。阮籍、嵇康不拘礼教、任性不羁、愤世嫉俗的人格表现，陶渊明"不为五斗米折腰"，而宁愿"采菊东篱下"的人生态度，甚至欧阳修流连山水时"醉翁之意不在酒，在乎山水之间也"的理想，无一不受庄子的影子。李白、苏轼面对人生的大起大落，能够不惊不乱，依然旷达自适，更可看出受庄子濡染之深。总之，庄子对中国文人精神的影响难以一语道尽，大到人格取向，小到细枝末节，都与庄子有着或多或

landscape literature, pastoral literature, and mystery literature. Li Bai in the Tang Dynasty was deeply influenced by Zhuangzi's romantic style of "opening up the magnificent and extraordinary words". His poems and essays are passionate, imaginative, magnificent and unrestrained, which form another peak of Chinese Romantic Literature after *Zhuangzi*. Su Shi of the Song Dynasty also got the true meaning of Zhuangzi's romanticism as he said, "I have seen it in my mind in the past, but I can't say it. When I read *Zhuangzi* now, I have found we think alike."(Seeing in Su Zhe's *Epitaph of My Brother Zizhan*)That shows Su Shi's natural, broad-minded and outstanding personality; His writings and thought in "Red Cliff Ode" and other notes like "Qingfeng Tower", "Towering Balcony", "Treasured Scrolls Hall", and "Detached Balcony" are all based on *Zhuangzi*. The style of his articles is similar to *Zhuangzi* which is "like flowing water" and "like gushing spring". Thus, he creates a school of Ci named "bold word".

Thirdly, the aesthetic thought in Zhuangzi's prose has a profound influence on Chinese literature and art. Zhuangzi thinks that "heaven and earth have their great beauties but do not speak of them." ("Zhi Traveling North") Beauty exists between heaven and earth and is owned by nature. With this understanding people believe that this thought directly gave birth to and promoted the development of Chinese landscape poetry, pastoral poetry, travel notes and other literary forms. Chinese painting and calligraphy are also influenced by it. Landscape painting has become the main type of Chinese painting for its beauty from heaven and earth. Influenced by its "great beauty" aesthetic sentiment and romantic style, calligraphy has produced cursive calligraphy, represented by Zhang Xu's and Huaisu's. Zhuangzi is also the only pioneer in aesthetics of "taking ugliness as beauty". He does not pursue the perfection of body, but spirit. Zhuangzi's aesthetic orientation of highlighting spiritual beauty by contrasting with body ugliness has become another source of inspiration for later writers and artists. Writers express their spiritual pursuit by "ugly stone" and "sick plum", while painters express their indomitable spiritual strength by weird and ugly figures. In addition, Zhuangzi's writing principles of meaning grasped but language forgotten, language plain while keynote profound, and meaning beyond words have a direct impact on many literati's literary theory and criticism thoughts, such as Liu Xie's "emotion is beyond words", Zhong Rong's "words may use up but the

少、或深或浅的联系。

　　第五，庄子思想对现代人的精神生活产生了很大的影响。在对待生死的问题上，庄子给出了旷达的人生境界。于人而言，有生一定会有死，这是不可改变的规律。他"把天地作为棺椁，把日月作为美玉，把星辰作为珠宝，万物都来陪葬。难道这么多的葬物还不算齐备吗？还有什么比这更好的呢？"的态度，让我们学会了豁达豪迈地面对生死。庄子超越物欲之困，提倡"无己""无功""无名"，不为物累，不为物役，保持精神的自由和心灵的宁静，也对后世产生了很大的影响。作为一位别具眼光和淑世情怀的圣贤先哲，庄子道论中所体现出的"道通为一""以道观之""道法自然""泛爱万物""逍遥无为"等思想，以及"养生论""生死论""自然美学论"等学说，都包含了中华民族传统哲学思想中伟大的人文情怀和深刻的"生态哲学"精神。它对于纠正西方工业革命以来现代人类所面临人与自然二元对立的世界观、单一经济指标的社会发展观、无限向自然索取的消费观、人类中心主义、因无度竞争而引发的战争危险等难题，都富有很好的启迪意义。

meaning is endless", Sikong Tu's "image beyond image, scenery beyond scene", Wang Guowei's "Realm Theory" and so on.

Fourthly, Zhuangzi's scorn of power and wealth, pursuit of independent and free personality and the spirit of carefree and self-adaptive make the Chinese literati have another life pursuit in addition to the Confucian "self-cultivation, regulating the family, governing the country and pacifying the world". Many of Chinese literati are influenced by Zhuangzi: Ruan Ji and Ji Kang's unruly and cynical personality, Tao Yuanming's life attitude of taking "the leisure way of life like picking chrysanthemums under the east fence" rather than "compromising to the superior" and Ouyang Xiu's ideal of "not drinking but caring about scenery between mountains and rivers" when he lingers in the mountains and rivers are all reflected by Zhuangzi. Facing the ups and downs of life, Li Bai and Su Shi are still broad-minded and self-adaptive, which shows the deep influence of Zhuangzi. In a word, Zhuangzi's influence on the spirit of Chinese literati can hardly be explained in a single word. From personality orientation to detailed ways of doing things, there is somewhat connection with Zhuangzi.

Fifthly, the thought of Zhuangzi has a great influence on modern people's spiritual life. On the issue of life and death, Zhuangzi takes a broad-minded realm of attitude toward life. As far as human beings are concerned, there must be death if there is life, which is an unchangeable natural law. He "takes heaven and earth as coffin, sun and moon as jade, stars as jewelry, and all things are buried with me. Aren't so many funeral objects enough? What could be better?" from which we may learn how to face life and death open-minded. Zhuangzi transcends the confinement of material desire, advocates "no self", "no merit", and "no fame", without the fetter of material servitude so as to maintain spiritual freedom and tranquility, which also have a great impact on later generations. As a sage with unique vision and way of benefiting human beings, Zhuangzi's many theories concerning Tao all reflect the great humanistic feelings and profound "ecological philosophy" in the traditional Chinese philosophy, such as his thoughts of "all things are one from Tao", "observe from Tao", "Tao follows nature", "all things are equal" and "absolute freedom of inaction", and his theory of "health preserving", "on life and death", "natural aesthetics" and so on. It is of great significance and inspiration to correct the world outlook of dualistic opposition between man and

庄子井旁边立有河南省重点文物保护单位"庄子故里"碑
Stele of "Zhuangzi's Hometown", key cultural relic protection site of Henan Province, next to the Zhuangzi Well

nature, the social development outlook of single economic index, the consumption outlook of unlimited demand from nature, anthropocentrism, and the danger of war caused by excessive competition.

第五章
庄子寓言50则

Chapter 5

Fifty Fables from Zhuangzi

1. 鹏程万里

这则寓言出自《庄子·逍遥游》。

北海里有一种大鱼,它的名字叫作鲲。鲲很大,不知道有几千里。鲲化而为鸟,名字叫作鹏,鹏的脊背,也不知道有几千里长。大鹏奋起高飞,它的翅膀就像遮盖天空的彩云。这只大鹏在海浪汹涌、海风大作的时候,就要飞到南海去。南海,就是天池。大鹏向南海迁移,翅膀在水面上激起3000里远的浪花,环绕着强烈的旋风,冲上九万里高空,半年后才在天池边停歇下来。

后来,人们就根据这个故事,编了一个成语"鹏程万里",用来比喻人奋发有为,前程远大。

2. 丽姬悔泣

这则寓言出自《庄子·齐物论》。

在丽戎国艾地守卫疆土的官员有一个宝贝女儿,名叫丽姬,长得很漂亮。晋国在征伐丽戎国时,俘获了丽姬,打算把她献给晋国的君主。丽姬感到非常害怕,非常痛苦,天天哭泣,把衣服都哭湿了。等她真的嫁过去后,生活在宫中,与君主一同睡在宽广华丽的床榻上,一起享受山珍海味的时候,丽姬感到非常快乐。想到当初自己哭得死去活来,丽姬感到非常后悔。

庄子用这个故事宣传"齐生死"的观念。古代女子在出嫁时不知道婚后的命运,所以出嫁时有"哭嫁"的风俗。庄子用这则寓言故事来类比人们眷恋生存,害怕死亡。这则故事客观上说明了人们对于陌生的事物往往感到害怕。

3. 鼓盆而歌

这则寓言出自《庄子·至乐》。

庄子的妻子死了,惠子来吊丧,却看见庄子正叉开两条腿,像簸箕

1. The Peng's Long Flight

This fable is from "Wandering in Absolute Freedom" of *Zhuangzi*.

There is a big fish in the North Sea whose name is Kun. Kun is so huge that no one knows how many thousands Li it measures. Kun turns into a bird which is named Peng whose back covers thousands Li. Rising to fly, Peng's wings are like clouds covering the sky. When the sea is moved, this bird Peng will prepare to the southern sea, the Celestial Pond. When the Peng is relocating to the southern sea, its wings stir up waves for 3000 Li. By a strong whirlwind, it is soaring to 90 thousands Li for half a year, and then stops at the edge of the Celestial Pond.

Later, according to this story, people make up an idiom "The Peng's Long Flight" to describe a person who works hard and has a bright future.

2. Lady Li Weeps with Regret

This fable is from "Making All Things Equal", *Zhuangzi*.

The official who guards the territory in Ai, Lirong state, has a beautiful daughter named Liji (Lady Li). When the state of Jin conquered Lirong, Liji was captured and going to be dedicated to the imperial monarch of the state of Jin. Liji felt very scared and miserable. She cried every day even got her clothes wet. After she really married to the monarch, living in the palace, sleeping on the broad and gorgeous bed and enjoying the delicacies with the monarch, Liji felt very happy. Recalling to her heartbreaking weeping before marrying, Liji felt very regretted.

Zhuangzi makes use of this story to promote the concept of "taking equal attitude toward life and death". In ancient times, women worried about their fate after marriage, so there was a custom of "weeping" when brides left their house and got married. Zhuangzi here makes an analogy for people's attachment to life and fear of death. This story objectively shows that people always fear the unknown things.

3. Pounding on a Tub and Singing

This fable is from "Supreme Happiness" of *Zhuangzi*.

When Zhuangzi's wife died, Huizi came to condole with him, but finding him squatting on the ground, with his legs sprawled out like a dustpan, pounding

似的坐在地上，一边敲着盆，一边唱着歌。

惠子很不理解，就对庄子说："你的妻子和你生活在一起这么多年，为你生儿育女，现在她不幸去世，你不哭也就算了，而你竟然还敲盆唱歌，这不是太过分了吗？"

庄子回答说："不是这样。当她刚死的时候，我自己是非常伤心难过的。可是细细想来，她起初本是无生命的，不仅没有生命，而且还没有形体。不仅没有形体，而且还没有气息，在若有若无、恍恍惚惚之间变化而有了生气，有了生气就变化而有了形体，形体再经过变化而有了生命，现在她又变化而死去，这种变化就像春夏秋冬四季那样运行不止，现在她静静地安息在天地之间，而我却还要号啕大哭，不是太不通达于命运吗，所以才止住不哭了。"

庄子用这个寓言故事宣传的也是"齐生死"的观念。庄子认为，人的生死如同四时的交替一样，是一种自然现象，表达了一种对于生死的达观态度。

4. 庄周梦蝶

这则寓言出自《庄子·齐物论》，是大家所熟悉的一则故事，也是庄子所提出的一个哲学命题。

庄子睡觉的时候，做梦梦见自己变成了一只美丽的蝴蝶，在天地之间翩翩飞舞，感到十分快乐与得意，全然不知道自己是庄子了。一会儿醒来，又在疑惑之中感觉自己就是庄子。但仔细一想，不知道是庄子做梦变成了蝴蝶，还是蝴蝶做梦变成了庄子。

这则故事虽然极其短小，但由于其渗透了庄子诗化哲学的精义，成了庄子诗化哲学的代表。庄子和蝴蝶肯定是有所区别的，这就叫作物我的融合与变化。庄子运用浪漫的想象力和美妙的文笔，通过对梦中变化为蝴蝶和梦醒后蝴蝶复化为己的事件的描述与探讨，提出了人不可能确切地区分真实与虚幻和生死物化的观点。这则故事由于包含了浪漫的思

a tub and singing.

Huizi didn't understand, so he asked for explanation, "Your wife has lived with you for so many years, and has given birth to children and brought them up for you, and then she has passed away. It's OK if you don't weep for her death, but you still sing. Don't you think that you're going too far?"

Zhuangzi explained, "Not so. When she just died, I was very sad. But when I ponder about it, she is inanimate at first, not only inanimate, but also formless. There is not only formless, but also no breath. In a trance, she changes and has vitality. With vitality, she changes and has body. Body changes and has life. Now she changes and dies. This kind of change is just like the four seasons of spring, summer, autumn and winter. Now she is resting quietly between heaven and earth, but I still have to cry, don't I understand the natural law? So I stop crying."

Zhuangzi uses this fable to promote the idea of "taking equal attitude toward life and death" as well. Zhuangzi believes that life and death of human beings are as usual as the natural phenomenon like the alternation of four seasons. That reflects his optimistic attitude towards life and death.

鼓盆而歌

Pounding on a Tub and Singing

想情感和丰富的人生哲学思考，引发后世众多文人骚客的共鸣，成了他们经常吟咏的题目，而最著名的莫过于李商隐所言"庄生晓梦迷蝴蝶，望帝春心托杜鹃"。

5. 邯郸学步

这则寓言出自《庄子·秋水》。

战国时期，燕国的寿陵有个少年，听人说赵国邯郸人走路的姿势很优美，于是不顾路途遥远，来到邯郸学习当地人走路的姿势。结果，他不仅没有学到邯郸人走路的姿势，还把自己原来走路的姿势也忘记了，最后只好爬着回去。

庄子用这个寓言故事告诉人们，如果一味地模仿别人，不仅学不到本领，反而把原来的本领也丢掉了。

6. 越俎代庖

这则寓言出自《庄子·逍遥游》。越，跨过；俎，古代祭祀时摆祭品的礼器；庖，厨师。主祭的人跨过礼器去代替厨师办席。比喻超出自己业务范围去处理别人所管的事。

原始社会时期，部落联盟酋长尧年纪大了，打算把天下让给道德高尚的许由，就说："日月出来了，而火炬还不熄灭，火炬要显示出光不是很难吗？及时雨已经下了，还需要人工灌溉，对于润泽禾苗不是徒劳吗？您如果担任天下领袖，一定会把天下治理得很好，我还在这儿占着这个位子，自感惭愧，请让我把天下送给你吧。"

许由说："您治理天下，天下已经完全安定，而我还要代替你，我是徒为其名吗？名，只是实的称谓而已，我何必要徒为其名？鹪鹩在深林里筑巢，所需不过一个树枝而已。偃鼠到河里饮水，所需不过满腹而已。您还是回去吧，不要劝我了。我要天下做什么呢？庖厨虽然不下厨，主持祭祀的人也不能越位去代替他。"

4. Zhuangzhou Dreaming As a Butterfly

This fable is chosen from "Making All Things Equal" of *Zhuangzi* in which the story is familiar to us, and contains a philosophical proposition proposed by Zhuangzi.

When Zhuangzi was sleeping, he dreamed that he had become a beautiful butterfly, dancing between heaven and earth. He felt very happy and proud, and did not realize that he was Zhuangzi at all. After a while, he woke up and wondered that maybe he was Zhuangzi. But pondered about it, he didn't know if he were Zhuangzi who had dreamed he was a butterfly or a butterfly dreaming he was Zhuangzi.

Although this story is extremely short, it has become the representative of Zhuangzi's poetic philosophy because it permeates the essence of Zhuangzi's poetic philosophy. There must be some difference between Zhuangzi and butterfly! This is called the transformation of things and self. By adopting the romantic imagination and wonderful writing style to depict and discuss the event of changing into a butterfly in dream and turning back into himself after waking up from the dream, Zhuangzi put forward that it is impossible for human beings to distinguish reality from illusion and life from death which originate from

庄周梦蝶
Zhuangzhou Dreaming As a Butterfly

庄子用这个寓言故事告诉人们,一个人的能力、认识、知识等都是有限的,应该按照自己的能力、认识、知识去做事,如果超过自己的能力、认识、知识之外,就不要再去做了。

7. 朝三暮四

这则寓言出自《庄子·齐物论》。

战国时,宋国有个名叫狙公的老人,十分喜爱猴子,就养了一大群猴子。狙公能理解猴子们的心意,猴子们也能够了解狙公的心思。狙公的家境并不富裕,但宁可省吃俭用,也要让猴子吃饱。

朝三暮四
Three at Dawn and Four at Dusk

猴子们很贪食。过了不久,家里食物就被猴子吃得剩下不多了。狙公不胜负担,打算限制猴子们的食物。一天,他对猴子们说:"明天起给你们吃栗子,早上给三个,晚上给四个,够了吗?"猴子们一听,都站了起来,十分恼怒。狙公见状便说:"好吧,那么就早上给四个,晚

transformation of things. This story contains romantic thoughts and feelings and rich philosophical thinking of life, which has aroused the resonance of many literati and poets in later generations, and has become a topic they often chant. The most famous one is Li Shangyin's poem "Zhuangzi loves to be a butterfly in his dreams; Emperor Wang rests his resentment on the cuckoos".

5. Learning How to walk in Handan

This fable is from "The Floods of Autumn", *Zhuangzi*.

During the Warring States period, there was a young man in Shouling of the state of Yan. He heard that the people of Handan in the state of Zhao had a beautiful walking posture, so regardless of the distant journeys, he came to Handan to learn the local people's walking posture. As a result, he not only failed to learn the walking posture of Handan people, but also forgot his own way of walking, and finally had to crawl back.

Zhuangzi wants to tell people by the fable that if one blindly imitates others, he will not only fail to acquire the new ability, but also lose his own acquired ability.

6. The Priest Overstepping the Duty of the Chef

This fable is from "Wandering in Absolute Freedom", *Zhuangzi*. Yue, overstepping; Zu, sacrificial vessels used in ancient China for offering sacrifices; Pao, cook or chef. The chief priest went to take the place of the chef. It refers to going beyond one's own business to deal with other people's affairs.

In the primitive society, Yao, the chief of the tribal alliance, was old and intended to resign the throne to Xu You, who had noble morality, "Isn't it a waste of light if the torch is still burning when the sun and the moon have already come out? Isn't it a waste of labor if one continues to water the fields when timely rains have been falling? If you were the leader, you will certainly run the country well. I feel ashamed of still occupying the position. Please let me hand over the throne to you."

Xu You replied, "Since you run the country, it has been in good order. If I were to take your place, would I be seeking after name? Name is just a reference to the object, so why would I seek for the name? The wren that builds a nest in

上给三个，这样够了吗？"猴子们听说早上的栗子加了一个，都非常高兴，纷纷趴在地上表示满意。

经典童话"猴子吃栗子"即源于此，大家在讥笑猴子傻的同时，还可以联想到权力分配及其管理学等方面的问题。

8. 魍魉问影

这则寓言出自《庄子·齐物论》。魍魉，意为人的幽灵。

幽灵问影子说："你原来是行走着的，现在你站住了；原来你是坐着的，现在你站起来了，你怎么这样没有独立的节操呢？"

影子说："我因为是有所依赖才这样的啊！我所依赖的，又要有所依赖才能活啊！我的行动是要依赖别的东西的，就像蛇的爬行需要依赖它腹部的横鳞，知了的飞行需要依赖它的翅膀一样啊！我怎么知道为什么一会儿这样，一会儿又不这样呢？"

这则寓言说明，幽灵之所以能责问影子，是因为影子只能随身体而动，没有属于自己的独立地位。而幽灵则相反，用不着依赖任何形体，能够无拘无束地到处游荡。这一事件本身说明了"形之存在"并非"影之存在"的必要条件。

9. 庖丁解牛

这则寓言出自《庄子·养生主》。

有一个名叫丁的厨师，人称庖丁。庖丁给梁惠王宰牛，技术高超，手法娴熟，游刃有余，刀子刺进去时的唰唰声，像音乐一样，合乎音律节奏。

梁惠王看得目瞪口呆，惊叹地说："啊!好极了!你宰牛的技术怎么会这样高超娴熟呢？"庖丁放下刀，回答说："我的爱好是探究事物的规律，这已经超过了对于宰牛技术的追求。当初我刚开始宰牛的时候，对于牛体的结构还不了解，看见的是完整的牛。三年后，见到的是牛的内

the deep forest occupies only a single branch; the mole that drinks from the river takes only a bellyful. You'd better go back and don't persuade me anymore. Why would I bother to rule the country? Even if the chef is not cooking, the priest in charge of the offering ceremony should not come to the kitchen to take the place of his duty."

Zhuangzi tries to tell us by this fable that we should do things according to our ability, cognition and knowledge which are limited, and things beyond which should not be done any more.

7. Three at Dawn and Four at Dusk

This fable is from "Making All Things Equal", *Zhuangzi*.

During the Warring States period, there was an old man named Jugong in the state of Song who loved monkeys very much and raised a large group of them. Jugong and the monkeys could communicate with each other very easily. Although his family was not rich, he would rather live frugally than let the monkeys suffer from hunger.

However, the monkeys were so greedy and gluttonous that the food had been almost eaten up by them after a while. So, Jugong had no way but let the monkeys on a diet, because he could not afford the food. One day, he told the monkeys, "I'll give you three chestnuts at dawn and four at dusk. Is it OK?" The monkeys all stood up angrily for objection. When he saw this, Jugong changed his mind and said, "Well, four in the morning and three in the evening. Is it OK?" On hearing that there was one more chestnut in the morning, the monkeys were all very happy, and lying down on the ground to show their satisfaction with this arrangement.

This is the origin of the classic fairy tale "Monkeys Eat Chestnuts". When we laugh at monkeys for being silly, we can also draw a lesson about power distribution and management and so on.

8. The Penumbra Asking the Shadow

This fable is from "Making All Things Equal", *Zhuangzi*. Wangliang means penumbra, the ghost of human beings.

The penumbra asked the shadow, "You used to be walking, but now you

部肌理筋骨，再也看不见整头的牛了。到了今天，我只是用精神去接触牛的身体就可以了，而不必用眼睛去观看。就像视觉停止活动了，而全凭精神意愿在活动。技术一般的厨工每月换一把刀，而我的这把刀已用了十九年了，宰的牛也有几千头，而刀刃还像刚从磨刀石上磨出来的一样。牛身上的骨节是有空隙的，刀刃并不厚，用这样薄的刀刃刺入有空隙的骨节，解牛时就显得游刃有余了，因此，用了十九年而刀刃仍像刚从磨刀石上磨出来一样。"

梁惠王说："好啊!讲得妙极了！我听了庖丁的话，学到了养生的道理了。"

这则寓言故事告诉我们，应该顺应自然以保身、全生、尽天年的养生之道。同时也说明了世上的万物虽然复杂，但都有自然规律可以遵循，只有反复实践，不断积累经验，才能掌握事物的规律，做到游刃有余。

10. 望洋兴叹

这则寓言出自《庄子·秋水》。

秋天来到，天降大雨，无数细小的水流，汇入黄河。只见波涛汹涌，河水暴涨，淹没了河心的沙洲，浸灌了岸边的洼地，河面陡然变宽，隔水远望，连河对岸牛马之类的大牲畜也分辨不清了。

眼前的景象多么壮观啊，河伯以为天下的美景都汇集到他这里来了，不由洋洋得意。他随着流水向东走去，一边走一边观赏风景。

后来，河伯来到北海边。他向大海那边望去，只见海上汪洋一片，无边无际，怎么也看不到头。河伯大吃一惊，不由得望洋兴叹，对海神若说："俗话说'听了很多道理，便认为没有谁能比得上'，说的就是我吧。而且我还曾听人说有人小看孔子的学识，轻视伯夷的行径，开始我不相信，如今我看到你浩瀚无边，不能穷尽，我若不是来到你的面前，那就危险了，我必将一直见笑于大方之家。"

stop walking; you used to be sitting, now you stand up. How could you be so changeable without independent discipline?"

The shadow retorted, "I'm doing so because there is something which I can depend on! What I depend on have to rely on something for a living! My action depends on something else, just like the snake's crawling depends on its abdominal scales, and cicada's flying depends on its wings! How can I know why I am so changeable?"

This fable shows us the reason why the penumbra can question the shadow is that the shadow can only move with the body but has no independent action of its own. The penumbra, on the contrary, can roam freely without depending on anybody or form. This event itself shows that "the existence of form" is not a necessary condition for "the existence of shadow".

9. Cook Ding Carving Bulls

This fable is from "Essentials for Keeping Good Health", *Zhuangzi*.

There was a cook named Ding who was invited to slaughter a bull for King Hui of the state of Liang. He was very skillful in using the knife to stab into the joints where there was more than enough space for the blade of knife, and the swish sound of cutting was like music in line with the rhythm.

King Hui of Liang was stunned and exclaimed, "Oh! Wonderful! How can you carve the bull so skillfully?" Cook Ding put down his knife, and replied, "I am interested in exploring the law of things, which has exceeded the pursuit of skill of slaughtering bulls. When I first started slaughtering bulls, what I could see was a complete bull without knowing the structure of it. Three years later, I could no longer see the complete bull; instead, I saw the inner texture, muscles and bones of bulls. Now, I just use the spirit but not eyes to touch the body of bulls. It seems that my eyes have stopped function, and the will of spirit is the only means by which to cut the bull. A mediocre cook changes his knife once a year, but I've had this knife for nineteen years to slaughter thousands of bulls with it, and yet the blade kept as sharp as though it had just come from the grindstone. That's because there are gaps in the joints of bulls, and the blade is not thick, so it is easy to use such a thin blade to pierce into the joints with gaps. Therefore, after nineteen years, the blade of my knife is still as sharp as when it first came from

这则寓言故事告诉我们，只有见了大世面，才能感觉到自己的渺小。

11. 浑沌开窍

这则寓言出自《庄子·应帝王》。

南海的神仙名字叫倏，北海的神仙名字为忽，中央的神仙为浑沌。倏与忽时常常一起相遇于浑沌之地，浑沌待他们很好。倏与忽商量要报答浑沌的恩德，说人皆有眼、耳、口、鼻等七窍，用来看东西，听声音，吃东西，呼吸，而浑沌却没有七窍，我们试着给他凿出来。于是每天凿一窍，凿到第七天，浑沌就死掉了。

这则寓言反映了庄子强调天道无为，反对把个人的主观愿望强加于客观事物的哲学观点。每个人都有自己的思想，你所喜欢的，别人不一定就喜欢。我们习惯于自以为是，常常会把自己的主观意愿强加给客观事物，强加给别人，结果就会出现好心办坏事的现象。

12. 不材之木

这则寓言出自《庄子·人间世》。

有个姓石的木匠到齐国去。经过曲辕的时候，看到社边有棵大栎树，树干可供一千头牛遮阴，树的周长有100多围，离地数十丈高才分树杈，这些枝条可以做几十条船。众人观看，如同集市。但姓石的木匠看也不看，头也不回，就走过去了。

弟子仔细观看后赶上他说："自从我拿起斧子跟您学艺，没有看到过这样好的木材，你却看也不看，直往前走，这是为什么？"

姓石的木匠回答说："算了，不要讲这棵树了。这是一棵木质松散的树，用它做成的船会沉没，用它做成棺材马上会腐朽，用它做成器具很快会毁坏，用它做成门窗会渗透黏液，用它做成柱子很快会生虫。这是一棵没有用的树，正是因为它没有用，所以寿命才长，才能长得这么高。"

the grindstone."

King Hui of Liang said, "Good! That is wonderful! I have learned how to preserve health from Cook Ding's sayings."

This fable tells us that we should conform to nature to acquire the Tao of preserving health in protecting the body, keeping alive, and live our full span of life. At the same time, it also shows that the complicated things in the world all follow the natural laws. Only by repeatedly practicing and accumulating experience can we master the natural laws and be able to do it with ease.

10. Sighing to the Sea

This fable originates from "The Floods of Autumn", *Zhuangzi*.

At the time of autumn floods, numerous streams poured into the Yellow River. The torrents of the river were so violent that the alluvion in the river and marsh land on the riverside were all swallowed by the torrents. With the river's suddenly widening, it was impossible to distinguish a horse from a cow looking on the other riverside.

What a magnificent sight he saw. Hebo thought that all the beautiful scenery in the world had come to him, and he couldn't help being complacent. He walked eastward to enjoy the scenery along the riverside.

Later, Hebo came to the north coast. He looked ahead to the other side of the sea, only to see a vast boundless sea with no end. Hebo was so surprised that he could not help sighing and said to the sea god, "As the saying goes, 'after hearing a lot of reasons, one may think he is superior to anyone else.' That is just made to satirize the people like me. Moreover, I have heard that some people belittled Confucius' knowledge and Boyi's behavior. At first, I didn't believe it. Now I see your unfathomable and boundless vastness. If I didn't come to see you, it would be dangerous for me, whom will be forever laughed at by the great masters."

This fable tells us that only when we see the greatness of the world, can we feel our own insignificance.

11. Boring for Chaos

This fable originates from "Competent Emperors and Kings", *Zhuangzi*.

The ruler of the southern sea was Shu (the Helter). The ruler of the northern sea was Hu (the Skelter) and the ruler of the central was named Hundun (Chaos).

庄子这则寓言，透露给我们的是"有用"与"无用"的观点。貌似强大的事物往往华而不实。看问题、观察事物不能被表面现象所迷惑，要透过现象看清本质，否则，就会做出错误的判断。

13. 藐姑射山神人

这则寓言出自《庄子·养生主》。

肩吾问连叔："我从接舆那里听到一些话，夸大得不合事理，一说下去就不能回到本题。我惊讶他的话，好像天上银河那样没有边际，和事实相差太远，不符合世间情理。"

连叔说："他说了什么话？"

肩吾说："他说：'在遥远的姑射山上，住着一个神人，皮肤如同冰雪一样洁白，姿态好像处女一样柔美；不吃各种食物，只食清风，只喝露水；她乘着云气，驾着飞龙，游在世界之外。她精神专注，使万物不受灾害，使粮食年年丰收。'我认为这是不合情理的。"

连叔说："是这样的。瞎子无法欣赏文采的美观，聋子无法欣赏钟鼓的乐声。难道只是人的形体有聋有瞎吗？心智上也是有聋有瞎的。这样的话，就是说你的啊。这个神人呀，她的德行，同万事万物混同为一体，使天下求得大治，怎能忙忙碌碌地把世间俗事作为自己的事务呢！这样的神人，一切外物没有什么能伤害她，滔天的洪水也不能淹没她，大旱高温使铁石融化、土山焦裂，她也不感到灼热。这种人看起来像尘垢秕糠般无大用之才，也还可以造就培养成为像尧、舜那样的圣贤人君，她怎能把管理具体事务作为自己的职责呢？"

这则寓言故事中的藐姑射山神人，是庄子幻想出来的绝对自由的人物形象。庄子把自由自在作为人生处世的理想境界，为了达到这一境界，庄子认为，必须与外物"无待"，即摆脱与外物的对立、依赖关系，而做到"无待"的关键就是"无己"。藐姑射山神人就是无己而逍遥的形象。

Shu and Hu often meet in the central place of chaos, and chaos was hospitable to them. Shu and Hu consulted to repay Chaos' kindness and hospitality, saying that every man has seven orifices such as eyes, ears, mouth and nose, which are used to see, hear, eat and breathe. However, Chaos did not have any of them, so let's try to bore them out for him. So they bored one orifice each day, and on the seventh day Chaos died.

This fable reflects Zhuangzi's philosophical point of view, which emphasizes that the way of heaven is inaction, but opposes imposing individual's subjective desire on objective things. Everyone has his own idea, what you like, others may dislike. We are used to being self-righteous which may often lead to imposing our subjective will on objective things and others. As a result, there comes the bad result with good intentions.

12. The Unusable Tree

This fable is from "Ways of the Human World", *Zhuangzi*.

A carpenter surnamed Shi went to the state of Qi on his way of passing Quyuan, where he saw an oak tree, which was used as the altar for the spirits of the land.

The tree was so large that it can shelter one thousand of bulls and can be measured one hundred of spans around. Only when it was tens of feet above the ground could it be divergent into branches, which could be made into dozens of boats. There were so many visitors stopped by the tree which made the place like a bazaar. But the carpenter Shi just walked over without even one glance at the tree.

After watching the tree carefully, Shi's disciple caught up with him and said, "Since I picked up the ax to learn from you, I had never seen such good wood, but you don't even look at it and go straight ahead. Why?"

The carpenter Shi replied, "Forget it. Don't talk about this tree anymore. This is a tree with loose wood. Used for making ships, the ships will sink; for Coffins, the coffins will soon decay; for utensils, they will soon be destroyed, for doors and windows, there will be mucus penetrating from them and for pillars, they will be soon bitten by worms. This is an unusable tree. It is just because it is unusable that it has a long life span and can grow so large."

The fable reveals to us the viewpoint of "being usable" and "being unusable".

14. 螳臂当车

这则寓言出自《庄子·人间世》。

鲁国有个贤人名叫颜阖，被卫灵公聘去当大公子的老师。但颜阖听说大公子德行败坏，跟他相处非常危险，于是就向卫国大夫蘧伯玉请教说："有一个人，假如我与他朝夕相处而不符合法度与规范，就会危害国家；如果合乎法度与规范，就会危害自身。您说，我该怎么办？"

蘧伯玉说："首先要端正自己。表面上最好是与他亲近点，而内心里最好是与他和顺点。但顺从他不要关系过密，疏导他不要太露心意。你不知道螳螂吗？螳螂奋起它的臂膀去阻挡滚动的车轮，却不知道自己根本阻挡不了!你不了解那养虎的人吗？他从不敢用活物去喂它，因为他担心扑杀活物会激起老虎的凶残本性。他也不敢用整个动物去喂饲老虎，因为他担心撕裂动物也会诱发老虎凶残的本性。老虎能向饲养它的人摇尾乞怜，是因为饲养人通晓老虎的禀性。而遭到老虎残杀的人，是因为他触犯了老虎的性情啊！"

这则寓言故事主要是形容那些不自量力的人，想阻拦根本阻拦不了的突发情况。

Things that seem powerful are often flashy without substance. Seeing problems and observing things, we should not be confused by superficial phenomena. We should see the essence through phenomena. Otherwise, we will make wrong judgments.

13. A Holy Man on the Faraway Mount Guye

This fable originates from "Essentials for Keeping Good Health", *Zhuangzi*.

Jianwu asked Lianshu, "I heard some sayings from Jieyu, which were unreasonably exaggerated and detached from the topic. I was startled at what he said which were interminable like the Milky Way in the sky, and quite unreasonable."

Lianshu asked, "What did he say?"

Jianwu replied, "He said, 'On the faraway mountain of Guye, there lived a holy man whose skin was as smooth and white as ice and snow, and her manner was elegant and delicate as that of a virgin; She did not eat any food, but only inhaled breeze and drank dew; She was wandering beyond the world by mounting the clouds and driving the flying dragon. She rides the clouds, drives the flying dragon, and swims outside the world. She can protect all things from disaster and secure every year a plentiful harvest year for human beings.' I don't think it's reasonable."

Lianshu answered, "Well, we can't expect a blind man to appreciate the beauty of elegant figures, and a deaf man to hear the music of bells and drums. Are deafness and blindness for the human body only? No, there are deafness and blindness in mind as well. You are in the second case. This holy man is striving for the great peace of the world by taking his virtue and the things as equal. How can he was bothered by the trivial worldly affairs! Nothing can hurt such a holy man: the greatest floods could not drown him, nor would he feel the greatest heats from the great drought and high temperature which can make the iron and stones melting, and dirt hills scorching. Such a holy man can cultivate wise kings like Yao and Shun even from the dust and chaff of no great use. How can he be bothered with the worldly affairs?"

The holy man in this fable was coined by Zhuangzi as the figure of absolute freedom. Zhuangzi regards freedom as an ideal state of life, in order to achieve

15. 呆若木鸡

这则寓言出自《庄子·达生》。

纪渻子为周宣王驯养斗鸡。过了十天,周宣王问:"斗鸡训练好了吗?"纪渻子说:"还没有训练好,斗鸡现在正虚浮骄矜自恃意气呢。"又过了十天,周宣王又问训练好没有。纪渻子回答"还不行。它仍然听见别的鸡啼叫就叫,看见别的鸡接近就跳。"再过十天,周宣王又问。纪渻子说:"还不行,它还是那么顾看迅疾,意气强盛。"

又过了十天,周宣王问,纪渻子回答说:"差不多了。别的鸡即使打鸣,斗鸡已不会有什么反应了,看上去像木鸡一样,它的德行真可说是完备了。"周宣王亲自去查看斗鸡,斗鸡看上去果然像只木头鸡了,可是它的精神全凝聚在内,别的鸡没有敢应战的,看见它就转身逃走了。

呆若木鸡,本来比喻精神内敛,修养到家。后来演变为比喻人呆木不灵,失去知觉的样子,也形容人因恐惧或惊讶而发愣的样子。

which, we must get rid of the opposition and dependent relationship between human beings and the external things, that is "no difference" and the key of "no difference" is "no self". The holy man on faraway mount Guye is the image of no self and absolute freedom.

14. A Mantis Trying to Stop a Chariot

This fable is from "Ways of the Human World", *Zhuangzi*.

There was a sage named Yan He in the state of Lu who was employed by Duke Ling of Wei to be the teacher of his eldest son. However, when Yan He heard that the eldest son was morally corrupt and it was very dangerous to get along with him, he consulted Ju Boyu, a senior official of the state of Wei, for advice, "There is a man, if I get along with him day and night, and do not conform to the laws and norms, it will harm the country; If it conforms to the laws and regulations, it will harm me. So what should I do?"

Ju Boyu said, "First of all, correct you. It is best to be close to him on the surface, and in your mind, it is best to harmonize with him. Follow him but don't be too close to him; persuade him but don't show too much direct intention to him. Don't you know the story of the mantis? The mantis raised its arms to stop the rolling wheel, but it didn't know that it could not stop it at all! Don't you know how the tiger breeder feed the tiger? He never dared to feed it with living animals because he was afraid that killing living animals would arouse the tiger's ferocious nature. He did not dare to feed the tiger with the whole animal, because he was afraid that tearing the animal would induce the tiger's ferocious nature as well. The reason why a tiger could fawn to its breeder was that the breeder knew the nature of the tiger. And the reason why a man was killed by the tiger was because he had violated the tiger's nature!"

This fable mainly describes those who overestimated themselves to stop the unexpected situation which wouldn't be stopped at all.

15. Concentrated like a Wooden Cock

This fable is from "Full Understanding of Life", *Zhuangzi*.

Ji Shengzi was training a gamecock for King Xuan of Zhou. Ten days went by, King Xuan asked, "Is the cock ready for a fight?" Ji said, "Not yet. It is now

16. 东施效颦

这则寓言出自《庄子·天运》。颦，皱眉。

越国的美女西施住在若耶溪的西岸，因为她美若天仙，人也善良，聪明，能干，所以大家都很喜欢她。而在若耶溪的东岸，住着一位丑女，名叫东施，是个又蠢又难看的女子。

有一次，西施因为心口疼痛，便皱着眉头，用手按住胸口，慢慢地在街上走，这时对面过来的东施看见了西施，她觉得西施这模样比平时更加漂亮了。回去之后，东施便学着西施的样子，双手捂着胸口皱起眉头，慢慢地在街上走。东施本来就长得很丑，现在还装模作样，就更加难看了，街上行人见了她这个样子，吓得东躲西藏，不敢看她。

后来人们就用"东施效颦"来比喻不知道人家的好处和本身的缺点在哪里，胡乱模仿。

东施效颦
Dongshi Imitating Xishi

vain and arrogant, and relies on its own vigor." Another ten days went by; King Xuan asked if the cock has being well trained. Ji answered, "Not yet. It is still quarrelsome to crow while the other cocks crow and jump when seeing other cocks approaching." After another ten days, when King Xuan asked what the training was going on, Ji replied, "Not yet. It's still looking around fiercely and domineering."

Ten days later, King Xuan asked that again, and Ji replied, "Almost finished. Even if other gamecocks crow, the cock will not react. It looks like a wooden cock that has a complete virtue." King Xuan went to check the gamecock by himself. The cock indeed looked like a wooden one, but its spirit was all concentrated in. The other gamecock didn't dare to fight and meet it, but turned and ran away.

Concentrated like a wooden cock originally refers to the spirit of introverted and the extreme of cultivation. However it was used later to describe people's numbness and unconsciousness, and also to depict people's stupefaction due to fear or surprise.

16. Dongshi Imitating Xishi

This fable is from "Movements of Heaven", *Zhuangzi*. Pin means frown.

Xishi, the beauty of the state of Yue, lived on the west bank of the Ruoye River. Because she is beautiful, kind, intelligent and capable, everyone likes her very much. On the east bank of the river, there lived an ugly woman named Dongshi, who was stupid and ugly.

Once, because of the pain in her heart, Xishi frowned, pressed her hand on her chest, and walked slowly down the street. At this time, Dongshi, who came from the opposite side, thought Xishi in this manner was much more beautiful than usual. When she went back, Dongshi learned from Xishi, covered her chest with her hands, frowned and walked slowly in the street. Dongshi was originally ugly, and now it was even uglier to imitate Xishi by pretending to have heartache. When people in the street saw her like this, they were so scared that they didn't dare to see her.

Later, people used the metaphor of "Dongshi Imitating Xishi" to describe people who blindly imitate others without knowing the exact advantages of others and their own shortcomings.

17. 螳螂捕蝉

这则寓言出自《庄子·山木》。

庄子在雕陵栅栏边游玩,看见一只怪鹊从南方飞来,翅膀有七尺宽,眼睛长一寸,碰到庄子的前额落在栗树上。庄子感到很奇怪,说:"这是什么鸟?翅膀大又飞不走,眼睛大又看不清。"于是提着衣服快步走过去,拿着弹弓等待它。这时,庄子发现一只知了在阴凉地休息,忘记了危险。螳螂用树叶遮掩,向知了发起了进攻。螳螂捕捉到了知了,却忘掉自身的危险。怪鹊趁机突袭了螳螂。庄子心里一惊,说:"啊!事物之间相互制约,利与害互相招致。"庄子于是丢掉弹弓往回跑,管山林的官员赶过来辱骂庄子。

庄子回去后三天都感到不愉快,蔺且问道:"先生为什么看上去不愉快呢?"庄子说:"我感于外物,却差点失掉了自我,看到污水时差点失去了清泉。况且我听先生说过,到一个地方,要服从那里的禁令。我在雕陵游玩,忘乎所以,一只怪鹊从我额前飞过,而我在栗林里差点忘掉了自身的安全。管理栗林的官员辱骂我,所以我感到不愉快。"

后来人们从故事中引申出"螳螂捕蝉,黄雀在后"的成语,用来比喻目光短浅,只贪图眼前利益而忽视背后隐藏的危险。

18. 运斤成风

这则寓言出自《庄子·徐无鬼》。斤,斧头。挥动斧头,风声呼呼。比喻手法熟练,技艺高超。

有一次庄子送葬,经过惠子的墓地。庄子回过头来对跟随的人说:"郢地有个人在自己的鼻尖上涂抹了白灰泥,像蚊蝇的翅膀那样大小细薄,这个人让匠石用斧子削掉这个小白点。匠石挥动斧子运斤成风,郢人听其挥削,鼻尖上的白泥完全除去而未伤着鼻子。郢人站在那里若无其事,不失常态。宋元君知道了这件事,召见了匠石说:'你为我也这么试试。'匠石说:'我确实曾经能够砍削掉鼻尖上的小白点。虽然

17. Mantis Catching the Cicada

This fable is from "A Mountain Tree", *Zhuangzi*.

Zhuangzi was wandering in the yard of Diaoling when he saw an extraordinary magpie flying from the south. Its wings were seven feet wide and its eyes were one inch long. It touched Zhuangzi's forehead and landed on a chestnut tree. Zhuangzi was very surprised and said, "What kind of bird is this? The wings are too big to fly, and the eyes are too big to see clearly." So he walked quickly carrying his clothes and waited for it with his catapult. At this time, Zhuangzi found a cicada resting in the shade, without discovering the danger of the attack from a mantis. The mantis covered with leaves, attacked and caught the cicada, but it didn't realize its own danger was approaching. The magpie took the opportunity to attack the mantis. On seeing this, Zhuangzi was startled to cry, "Oh！Things restrict each other, and benefit and harm always come together." On comprehending this reason, Zhuangzi dropped the catapult and ran back. On his way back, the official in charge of the mountain forest came to abuse Zhuangzi.

Zhuangzi was being unhappy for three days after he returned. Lin Qie asked, "Why are you unhappy, sir?" Zhuangzi replied, "I was affected by external things, but almost lost myself, just like I almost lost my clear spring when seeing the waste water. Besides, I've learned from you that when you go to a new place, you have to obey the ban there. However, when I was playing in Diaoling, I forgot your teaching. When there was a strange magpie flowing past my forehead, I almost forgot my own safety in the chestnut forest. The official in charge of the forest insulted me, so I didn't feel happy."

Later, the idiom "When a mantis is trying to catch a cicada, the yellow magpie is behind" is used to refer to shortsightedness, greed for immediate interests and neglect of hidden dangers.

18. Whirling Axe with Noise like Wind

This fable is from "Xu Wugui", *Zhuangzi*. Jin, axe. Wave the axe and the wind blows. That is an analogy to mean the master hand of the craftsman.

Once Zhuangzi was passing by Huizi's tomb when he attended a funeral ceremony. Zhuangzi turned back to tell his followers, "There was a man in Yingdi who smeared white mud on the tip of his nose, which was as thin as the wings of

如此,但是能够让我砍削的对象已经死去很久了。'自从惠子离开了人世,我没有可以匹敌的对手了!我也没有能够与之论辩的人了!"

"运斤成风"意为手法熟练,技艺高超,而匠人能够运斤成风,需要胆大的郢人配合。惠子是庄子的朋友,也是辩论对手,惠子死后,庄子失去了对手和知音。

19. 濠梁观鱼

这则寓言出自《庄子·秋水》。

庄子与惠施在濠水的桥梁上观鱼。庄子见水里的鱼自由自在地游来游去,便向惠施感叹道:"你看这些鱼无忧无虑,自由自在,鱼也有鱼的快乐啊!"惠施一听不以为然,马上反驳庄子:"你不是鱼,怎么知

濠梁观鱼

Fish Watching on the Bridge of the Hao River

a mosquito and a fly. This man asked carpenter Shi to cut off the little white spot with an axe. Carpenter Shi whirled an axe with noise like wind. When the man of Ying heard the sound, the white mud on the tip of his nose had completely been removed without hurting his nose. The man of Ying stood there as usual as if nothing had happened. When Duke Yuan of Song heard that, he summoned the carpenter and said, 'Try it for me.' Shi replied, 'I really used to be able to cut off the white spots on the tip of noses. But the man who trusted me and let me chop had been dead for a long time.' Since Huishi died, there is no close opponent whom I can argue with!"

"Whirling Axe with Noise like Wind" shows the skillfulness of the carpenter who needs the cooperation of such a brave man of Ying to present his master hand. Huizi was Zhuangzi's friend and opponent. After Huizi died, Zhuangzi lost his opponent and confidant.

19. Fish Watching on the Bridge of the Hao River

This fable is from "The Floods of Autumn", *Zhuangzi*.

Zhuangzi and Huishi were watching fish on the bridge of the Hao River. Seeing the fish swimming freely in the water, Zhuangzi sighed to Huishi, "Look, these fish are carefree, and they have their own happiness!" Huishi immediately refuted Zhuangzi, "You are not a fish, how can you know the happiness of fish?" Zhuangzi retorted at once, "You are not me, how can you know that I don't know the happiness of fish?" Huishi said, "I'm not you, and of course I don't know you. But you are not a fish neither, you must not know the happiness of fish." Zhuangzi argued again, "You just said, 'how do you know the happiness of fish since you are not a fish'. That means you already know me." Since you know me, why don't I know fish? I know the happiness of fish on the bridge!"

Zhuangzi and Huishi are good friends and debaters. The reason why Zhuangzi thinks that the fish is happy lies in his experience way of "seeing things from self". Namely, since Zhuangzi is happy when he is watching the fish, so he thinks that the fish is happy as well.

20. Obtaining a Valuable Pearl from the Black Dragon

This fable is from "Lie Yukou", *Zhuangzi*.

道鱼的快乐呢？"庄子立刻反问一句："你不是我，怎么知道我不知道鱼的快乐呢？"惠施说："我不是你，当然不知道你。但你也不是鱼，一定也不知道鱼的快乐。"庄子又辩道："你刚才说'你不是鱼，怎么知道鱼的快乐呢'，就说明你已经知道我了。既然你已经知道我，我怎么不知道鱼呢？我就是在桥上知道了鱼的快乐啊！"

庄子与惠施是好朋友，也是辩手。庄子认为鱼是快乐的，主要是采用了"以我观物"的体验方式，因为庄子观鱼的时候心情是快乐的，所以就认为鱼也是快乐的。

20. 探骊得珠

这则寓言出自《庄子·列御寇》。

有人去拜见宋王，宋王赏赐他十辆车，他便用这十辆车在庄子面前炫耀。庄子说："很久以前，黄河边上有一户人家，靠割芦苇编帘子为生，日子过得非常贫困。有一天，儿子在河边割芦苇，当他坐下来休息时，望着粼粼波光的河水，想起父亲说过，在河的最深处有许多珍宝，可是谁也不敢去，因为那里住着一条凶猛的骊龙。他想，要是潜到河底，找到珍宝，一家人就用不着像现在这样辛勤劳作而日子还过得十分贫穷。于是，他把心一横，脱了衣服，一头扎进河里，终于寻得一颗价值千金的宝珠。父亲见了宝珠，对儿子说：'好险哪！这颗价值千金的宝珠是长在骊龙嘴巴里的，你摘它的时候骊龙必定是睡着了。它要是醒着，你可就没命了。'如今的宋国深重莫测，不亚于九重深渊。宋王的威猛不亚于骊龙，你得到他的车，一定是遇到宋王睡着了，当宋王醒来，你不被粉身碎骨才怪。"

"探骊得珠"，意为冒大险得大利，得大利也就肯定有大险。后常比喻文章含义深刻，措辞扼要，得到要领。

21. 得鱼忘筌

这则寓言出自《庄子·秋水》。筌，捕鱼的竹器，竹篓子。

Someone went to pay a visit to the king of the state of Song. The king rewarded him with ten chariots, so he used them to show off in front of Zhuangzi. Zhuangzi said, "Once upon a time, there was a family on the side of the Yellow River who lived in poverty by cutting reeds and weaving curtains. One day, the son in the family was cutting reeds by the river. When he sat down to have a rest, staring at the sparkling river and recalled his father told him that there were many treasures in the deepest bottom of the river, but no one dared to go, because there lived a fierce black dragon. He thought that if he went down to the bottom of the river and found the treasure, his family would not have to work so hard and live in poverty. So he took off his clothes and dived into the river. Luckily enough, he found a valuable pearl at last. When the father saw the pearl, he told his son, 'How dangerous! This valuable pearl was in the mouth of the black dragon. When you picked it, the dragon must be asleep. If the dragon was awake, you would have died.' Now the state of Song is no less than the nine-fold abysses, whose depth is unpredictable. The king of Song is no less powerful than the black dragon. When you got his chariots, he must fall asleep and if he waked up then you would be broken into pieces without doubt."

"Obtaining a Valuable Pearl from the Black Dragon" means to take great risks and make great profits, and if you get great profits, there will be great risks. It is later taken as a metaphor to mean the writer can catch the key point of writing an article with profound meaning and concise wording.

21. Discarding the Trap after Catching the Fish

This fable is from "The Floods of Autumn", *Zhuangzi*. Quan, the bamboo trap or basket used for fishing.

A fisherman came to the river, threw Quan into the river, and soon caught the fish. He happily took the fish out of the Quan and went home, leaving it in its original place. When he got home, the fisherman showed off the fish to his wife. His wife asked him, "Where is the Quan?" Then the fisherman just remembered that he only took care of the fish, but forgot the Quan, the trap used for fishing.

Zhuangzi wants to remind us of remembering original object on which we relied to gain success by this story. Later, it is also used as a metaphor to describe ingratitude of the one after reaching the goal.

渔夫来到河边，把捕鱼的竹筌投进河里，很快就捕捉到了鱼。渔夫见到鱼，便高兴地把鱼取出来就回家了，把竹筌留在原处。回家后，渔夫把鱼拿出来向妻子炫耀。妻子问他："竹筌在哪里？"渔夫这才想起来，自己只顾及鱼，而忘记了捕鱼的竹筌。

庄子用这则故事形象地比喻事情成功以后，就忘了本来所依靠的东西。后来也比喻达到目的后而忘恩负义。

22. 鹓雏腐鼠

这则寓言出自《庄子·秋水》。鹓雏，中国古代传说中的五凤之一，被认为是一种瑞鸟，身为金色或黄色，又常用以比喻有才望的年轻人。

惠施在梁国做了相国，庄子听说以后就去见他。有人对惠施说："庄子这次来，是想取代你的相位。"惠施听说后，十分担心这件事，就在都城中搜捕庄子，竟然搜了三天三夜。

庄子听说后，就主动去见惠施，说："南方有种鸟叫鹓雏，你知道吗？这种鸟由南海起飞，飞到北海，不是梧桐树绝不下来休息，不是干净的果子绝不吃，不是甘美的泉水绝不饮用。在这时，有只鸱鸮得到了一只死老鼠，正在吃，见鹓雏飞过，害怕鹓雏夺走它的死老鼠，抬起头，看着鹓雏发出'吓吓'的声音。现在你想用你的梁国相位来'吓'我吗？"

庄子将自己比作鹓雏，是志向高洁之士，将惠施比作鸱鸮，把功名利禄比作腐鼠，表明自己鄙弃功名利禄的立场和志趣，讽刺惠施醉心于功名利禄且无端猜忌别人的丑态。庄子没有直言痛斥惠施，而用讲故事的方式来使惠施自己觉得愧疚，收到既尖锐痛快又余味不尽的效果。需要说明的是，庄子和惠施本是好朋友，惠子先于庄子而逝，庄子在《徐无鬼》篇中表达了对惠施的怀念。

22. Yuanchu and Rotten Rat

This fable is from "The Floods of Autumn", *Zhuangzi*. Yuanchu, one of the five phoenixes in ancient Chinese legend, is considered to be a kind of auspicious bird in golden or yellow color, and is often used to refer to talented young man.

Huishi became prime minister in the state of Liang, and Zhuangzi went to see him when he heard about it. Someone told Huishi, "Zhuangzi is coming to replace your position this time." Huishi took this seriously. He was very worried about it and searched Zhuangzi for three days and three nights in the capital of Liang.

And after hearing about that, Zhuangzi came to Huishi's house and told him, "There is a kind of bird in the South called Yuanchu, and I wonder whether you know it? This noble bird flies from the South Sea to the North Sea, and on its trip, it would not rest if it is not on Wutong tree, not eat if it is not clean fruit and not drink if it is not the sweet spring water either. At this time, there was a hawk who was eating a rotten rat as the Yuanchu passed by, the hawk was so scared and worried about the Yuanchu may take his food away, so he raised his head, looked up at Yuanch, and screamed, 'Shoo, shoo'! Now are you trying to shoo me with your position of prime minister of Liang?"

Zhuangzi compared himself to Yuanchu, who was a noble minded man, and compared Huishi to the hawk, and the fame and fortune were just like the rotten rat, which were disdained by Zhuangzi. By that metaphor it is to satirize Huishi's infatuation with fame and fortune and his unwarranted suspicion of others. Zhuangzi didn't directly denounce Huishi, but telling stories to make Huishi feel guilty, which had a sharp and lasting effect. It should be noted that Zhuangzi and Huishi were good friends. Huizi died before Zhuangzi and Zhuangzi expressed his nostalgia for Huishi in "Xu Wugui".

23. The Fight Between the State of Man and Chu

This fable is from "Zeyang", *Zhuangzi*.

Dai Jinren told the king of Wei that "There is a small animal called snail, your majesty, do you know it?"

The king of Wei said, "Yes."

Dai Jinren continued, "There is a country on top of the left tentacle of the

23. 蛮触之争

这则寓言出自《庄子·则阳》。

戴晋人对魏王说:"有叫蜗牛的小动物,国君知道吗?"

魏王说:"知道。"

戴晋人说:"有个国家在蜗牛的左角,名字叫触氏;另一个国家在蜗牛的右角,名字叫蛮氏。这两个国家时常为争夺土地而打仗,倒下的尸体数也数不清,追赶打败的一方花去整整十五天方才撤兵而回。"

魏王说:"啊!那都是虚妄的言论吧?"

戴晋人说:"让我为你证实这些话。你认为宇宙四方、上下有尽头吗?"

魏王说:"没有止境。"

戴晋人说:"您知道,同想象中的无限空间相比,再回头看看我们能到达的地方,这狭小的空间恐怕就像是若存若失一样吧?"

魏王说:"是的。"

戴晋人又说:"人们能到达的地方有一个魏国,魏国有一个大梁城,大梁城里有大王您。大王您与那蛮氏相比,有区别吗?"

魏王回答说:"没有区别。"

戴晋人辞别而去,魏王心中无限怅然,若有所失。

庄子讲这个故事主要是为了说明人的视野要远大,不要因细小而发生争端。

24. 大钩巨缁

这则寓言出自《庄子·外物》。

任国公子做了个大的钓鱼钩,系上了粗大的黑绳作钓绳,用五十头阉割后的牛做鱼饵,蹲在会稽山上,把钓竿投入东海,每天都这样钓鱼,整整一年一条鱼也没钓到。不久,一条大鱼吞食鱼饵,拉着巨大的钓钩,急速沉没海底,又急速地扬起脊背腾身而起,掀起如山的白浪,

snail whose ruler is called Chu, and on top of its right tentacle there is a state whose ruler is called Man. The two states often fight to control territory and go into wars with tens of thousands of corpses left on the ground. The victors have to chase for fifteen days before they return home."

The king of Wei said, "Oh! That sounds all nonsense, isn't it?""

Dai Jinren said, "Let me confirm that for you. What do you think of the universe ? Is there an end for each direction?"

The king of Wei said, "There is no end."

Dai Jinren said, "Well, compared with the imaginary infinite space in the universe, looking back at the places we can reach, and I'm afraid that this small space of Chu and Man is just like a drop in the bucket, right?"

The king of Wei approved, "Yes."

Dai Jinren continued, "Where can people reach there is a state of Wei, in which there is a capital city Daliang, and in Daling, there is a king of Wei, that is you, your majesty. Is there any difference between your majesty and the ruler of Man?"

The king of Wei replied, "No difference."

When Dai Jinren left, the king of Wei felt very sad and ill at ease.

Zhuangzi borrows this story mainly to show that people should have a broad vision and should not have disputes on some insignificant things.

24. An Enormous Fishhook with a Huge Line

This fable is from "External Things", *Zhuangzi*.

When a son of the duke of state Ren was fishing, he took a great fish hook with a huge black line, used 50 cattles of castration as bait, squatted on Kuaiji Mountain and cast a pole into the East Sea. For a whole year, he caught nothing. A year's later, a huge fish swallowed the bait and dragged the huge hook and plunged into the bottom of the sea in no time, and suddenly, rose up and shook its dorsal fins until the white wave of the sea was as high as a mountain, and the sea waters lashed and churned violently, roaring like ghosts and gods, shocking people that lived in thousands of miles away.

This huge fish could make everyone in the east of Qiantang River to the north of Jiuyi Mountain have a good meal. After that, those shallow and

海水剧烈震荡，吼声犹如鬼神，震惊千里之外。

任公子钓得这样一条大鱼，将它剖开制成鱼干，从钱塘江以东，到九嶷山以北，没有谁不饱饱地吃上这条鱼的。这以后那些浅薄之人和喜好品评议论之士，都大为吃惊地奔走相告。他们举着钓竿丝绳，奔跑在山沟小渠旁，守候小鱼上钩，至于想得到大鱼那就很难很难了。

庄子借这个故事说明人要有远大的抱负，才能成就大业。如果目光短浅，只顾及眼前利益，终会收获甚微。

25. 智有所困

这则寓言出自《庄子·外物》。

宋元君半夜梦见有人披着头发从侧门偷看，对他说："我来自叫宰路的深渊，替清江水神出使河伯住所，现在被渔人余且捕捉了。"元君醒来后，派人占梦。卜者说："这是只神龟。"元君问："渔人中有叫余且的人吗？"大臣们说有。元君说："要余且来见我。"

第二天余且来朝，元君问余且捕鱼有什么收获？余且回答说："我捕得一只白龟，周长五尺。"元君说："把你的白龟献上来。"白龟送到后，元君想杀它，又想放它，拿不定主意，就去占卜。卜辞说："杀龟用来占卜吉利。"于是把白龟剖开挖空，用龟板占卜数十次推断起来也没有一点失误。

孔子知道后说："神龟能托梦元君，而不能避开余且的捕捉。白龟的智慧能占卜七十二次没有失误，却不能避免掏肠挖肉之苦。如此看来，即使聪明也有穷尽的时候，神灵也有考虑不到的事情，即使聪明绝顶，也逃不过众人的谋算。鱼儿即使不畏惧渔网却也会害怕鹈鹕。摒弃小聪明方才显示大智慧，除去矫饰的善行方才能使自己真正回到自然的善性。婴儿生下地来没有高明的老师指教也能学会说话，只因为跟会说话的人自然相处。"

庄子通过料事如神的神龟却算不到自己的命运的故事，说明知识无边，智慧无穷，聪明的人也有考虑不周的事。

overcritical people were startled and rushed to tell each other the magic story of fishing. They were just holding the fishing rod and wire rope, running in the small ditch, and waiting for the small fish to take the bait. How could they catch the huge fish?

Zhuangzi uses this story to illustrate that only when people have lofty aspirations can they achieve great achievements. If one was short-sighted and only focus on immediate interests, he will gain little in the end.

25. No One Is Wise All the Times

This fable is from "External Things", *Zhuangzi*.

In the middle night, Duke Yuan of Song dreamed that someone was peeping through the side door with his hair disheveled down, saying, "I come from the abyss called Zailu. When I was sent to the residence of Hebo for a diplomatic mission for the water god of the Qingjiang River, I'm captured by the fisherman Yu Qie."Duke Yuan woke up and sent someone to divine by interpreting his dream. The diviner said, "This is a holy turtle." Duke Yuan asked, "Is there a fisherman named Yu Qie?" Ministers answered yes. Duke Yuan sent an order, "Bring Yu to see me."

The next day, Yu came, Duke Yuan asked him what he got from fishing. Yu Qie replied, "I caught a turtle, five feet in circumference." Duke Yuan ordered, "Give me your turtle." When the turtle was brought, Duke Yuan could not decide whether to kill it or let it go, so he consulted his diviners. On Oracle Inscriptions, it was said, "Killing the turtle for divination will bring good luck." So the turtle had its shell removed and made for divination dozens of times, and there was no failure at all.

Confucius heard the story and commented, "The turtle can make a request in Duke Yuan's dream, but it can't escape from Yu Qie's capture. Its shell can be used for divination for 72 times without mistakes, but it can't escape from the pain of being stripped of its shell. So there is no one who can be wise all the times; even the gods make no exceptions. Even if one is extremely wise, it can't escape the scheming of the multitude. Fish are afraid of pelicans even if they are not afraid of nets. Only by abandoning petty wisdom can we show great wisdom, and only by removing the pretentious good deeds can we truly return to the natural goodness.

26. 轮扁斫轮

这则寓言出自《庄子·天道》。

齐桓公在堂上读书，轮扁在堂下制造车轮。轮扁放下木工工具，到堂上去，问桓公："请问您读的那本书都说些什么？"桓公回答说："圣人之言。"轮扁问："圣人还在吗？"桓公说："已经死了。"轮扁说："既然如此，那么您读的不过是古人的糟粕而已。"桓公说："我读书，做车轮的匠人怎么能随便议论呢？你说得有道理则罢了，说得没有道理就要你的命。"轮扁回答说："我是臣子，我从自己从事的工作来看，凿车轮，孔宽缓了就松滑而不牢固，紧了就涩滞而难入。不宽不紧，就会得心应手，用口无法说明，但有技巧存在于其中。我不能把做轮子的技术给我的儿子讲明白，我的儿子不能从我这里接受这些技术。所以我活了70岁，还一直在制造车轮。古人同他们那不能传给后人的技巧和经验一起死掉了，既然如此，那么您所读的不就是古人的糟粕吗？"

庄子借这则寓言强调了实践的重要性，认为技巧的形成在于长期的积累。同时，庄子对儒家的思想观点有不同看法，且时有批评。

27. 坎井之蛙

这则寓言出自《庄子·秋水》。

坎井之蛙对东海之鳖说："我真快乐啊！我出来在井栏上跳跃，进去在残破的井壁边休息。到水里游泳，水刚刚到我的腋窝和下巴。到泥中跳跃，泥水刚刚淹没我的脚背，回过头来看看那些虾、蟹、蝌蚪，没有谁能比得上我。况且我独占了一坑水，叉开腿立在浅井中有乐趣，这也就快乐到极点了。先生，你为什么不常常进到井里来看看呢？"

东海之鳖左脚还未踏入井中，右膝就被绊住了，于是它犹豫了一会儿，退了出来，告诉坎井之蛙大海的情况，说："千里远，说明不了大海的大。千仞深，形容不尽大海的深。夏禹时，十年九涝，海水看不出

Babies are born to learn how to speak without a good teacher, just because they get along with people who can speak naturally."

Zhuangzi tells the story about the holy turtle, who is a god of foresight, but it can't count its own fate. It shows that knowledge is boundless; wisdom is infinite; the wise men are not always wise and considerate all the time.

26. Bian the Wheelwright Chiseling a Wheel

This fable is from "The Way of Heaven", *Zhuangzi*.

When Duke Huan of Qi was reading in the hall, Bian the wheelwright was chiseling a wheel under the hall at the same time. Bian put down his woodworking tools, went to the hall and asked Duke Huan," May I know what you are reading?" Duke Huan replied, "The sage's sayings." Bian made a detailed inquiry, "Is the sage still alive?" Duke Huan answered, "He's dead." Bian said, "That is to say what you read is just the dregs of the ancients." Duke Huan said with a discontented tone, "When I am reading, how dare the wheelwright to make comment casually and impolitely? It is tolerant if your sayings are reasonable, but if it is unreasonable, I will kill you."Bian replied, "I'm a minister. From my point of view as a wheelwright, if I proceed gently and slowly, the spokes will be loose and the wheel may not be safe; if I work quickly the spokes will be too tight and hard to fit. If the movements are neither too gentle nor violent, the idea in my mind can be realized through my hand. However the technology can't be explained with words, but kept in my mind. I can't explain and teach the technology of making wheels to my son, who can never get it. So I lived for 70 years and I've been chiseling wheels all the time. The ancients died together with their skills and experiences which could not be passed on to later generations. In this case, what you read is just the dregs of the ancients, isn't it?"

Zhuangzi, by this fable, emphasizes the importance of practice and believes that the formation of skills depends on long-term accumulation. At the same time, Zhuangzi has different views on Confucianism, and sometimes criticizes it.

27. The Frog in the Well

This fable is chosen from "The Floods of Autumn", *Zhuangzi*.

The frog in the well talked with a turtle from the East Sea, "I'm so happy!

增多。商汤时，八年七旱，海水看不出减少。海水不因为旱涝时间的短暂和长久而发生变化，不因为水量的多少而涨落，这也就是住在东海的一大快乐啊！"坎井之蛙听了这句话，吃惊，恐惧，手足无措，若有所失。

这则寓言故事，后演变成"井底之蛙"的成语。这则寓言通过井蛙在东海之鳖面前夸海口的故事，讽刺了那些鼠目寸光，孤陋寡闻，只能看到井口那么大的一块天却又狂妄自大的人。

28. 庄子借粮

这则寓言出自《庄子·外物》。

有一段时间，庄子家里贫困，无米下锅，无奈之下便去向监河侯借粮食。监河侯不肯借粮，就装出为难的样子说："庄子啊，我家里的粮食也不多了，我即将收取封邑之地的税金，到时候我借给你三百金，你看怎么样？"

庄子听了脸色骤变，气愤地说："我昨天来的时候，突然听到半道上有呼喊的声音。我循着声音走过去，发现在车轮碾过的小水坑里有条鲫鱼在那里挣扎，小水坑里的水已经不多了。我问道：'鲫鱼啊，你在这里干什么呢？'鲫鱼回答说：'快救救我吧，我是来自东海的鲫鱼，你能给我一升水使我活下来吗？'我对鲫鱼说：'鲫鱼啊，你不要着急，我这就到南方去，说服吴王和越王，请他们引西江之水到这里来，再把你接到东海老家去，你看可以吗？'鲫鱼听了脸色大变，气愤地说：'我失去了有水的生存环境，所以现在没有容身之所了，我只要能得到一升的水就可以活下来。可是你却非要这样做，还不如早点到卖干鱼的市场上去找我，或许还能找到我。'"

庄子借这则寓言讽刺了社会上假慷慨、真吝啬的伪君子。俗话说，远水解不了近渴，做事、做人都应该少说空话才是。

I came out to jump on the well fence and went in to rest beside the broken well wall. Swimming in the water, the water just reached my armpit and chin. Jumping in the mud, the muddy water has just submerged my insteps. Looking back at the shrimps, crabs and tadpoles, no one can match me. What's more, I monopolize the fun of standing in a shallow well with my legs apart, which is the extreme fun. Why don't you come in the well and have a look?"

Before his left foot entered the well, the turtle in the East Sea tripped over his right knee. So he hesitated for a while and stepped back to tell the frog about the sea, "Thousands of miles in length can't show the size of the sea. Thousands of rens (towering) in height can't compare with the depth of the sea. During the reign of King Xia and Yu, there were nine floods in ten years, and it seemed that there was no increase of sea water. In the reign of King Tang of the Shang Dynasty, there were seven droughts in eight years, and it seemed that there was no decrease of sea water. The sea water doesn't change because of the short and long time of drought and flood, and it doesn't fluctuate because of the amount of water. This is a great pleasure to live in the East Sea! "On hearing this, the frog was startled, frightened and at a loss.

This story later was coined into an idiom "A Well Frog", which was used to satirize those shortsighted, ignorant and arrogant people who can only see a sky as big as the well.

28. Zhuangzi Borrowing Grain

This fable is from "External Things", *Zhuangzi*.

For a time, Zhuangzi's family was so poor that they even had no food for living, so he went to the Marquis of Jianhe to borrow some grain. Marquis Jianhe didn't want to lend him grain, so he pretended to be in a dilemma and said, "Zhuangzi, I don't have much food in my family, but I'm going to collect taxes on the land of my fiefdom, and then I'll lend you 300 gold. Will that be all right?"

Zhuangzi flushed with anger and said, "When I was coming here yesterday, I heard someone calling me on the road suddenly. I followed the sound and found a carp struggling in the small puddle where the wheel ran over. There was not much water in the puddle. I asked, 'Carp, what are you doing here?' The carp replied, 'Please help me. I'm a carp from the East Sea. Can you give me a liter of water to

29. 天机所动

这则寓言出自《庄子·外物》。

一只脚的夔对多足虫蚿说:"我用一只脚跳着走,没有比我还能行走的了,现在你用一万只脚怎么个走法呢?"多足虫蚿说:"不是这样的,你没有看见咳唾的人吗?喷出的唾沫大的像珠子,小的像水雾,相杂而下,数都数不清。我是在本能的驱使下行动,说不清其中的缘由。"多足虫蚿对蛇说:"我用那么多的脚行走,还不如你没有脚快,这是为什么呀?"蛇说:"行动出于本能,怎么能更改呢?我哪里用得着脚呢?"蛇对风说:"我扭动脊背和两侧行走,好像是用脚。你呼啦啦从北海刮到南海,却好像没有利用什么,这是什么缘故?"风说:"是啊,我呼啦啦从北海刮到南海,但用手指遮挡我,用脚踢我,都能胜过我,我没有办法对付这些。即使这样,刮断大树,吹倒高楼,只有我才行,对付小的我没办法,对付大的我却还行。战胜大的只有圣人才行啊。"

庄子借这则寓言说明了任何事物都有自己与生俱来的特性,各有所长,顺其自然就能用其所长。

30. 舐痔得车

这则寓言出自《庄子·列御寇》。

宋国有个叫曹商的人,宋王派他出使秦国。曹商出发时,宋王赐给他几辆马车。到了秦国,秦王喜欢他,又赐给他一百辆马车。

返回宋国后,曹商见到庄子,向庄子炫耀说:"居住在偏僻狭小的巷子里,穷困窘迫,靠编织草鞋为生,饿得面黄肌瘦,那些是我曹商不如你的地方。一旦有机会见到了万乘之主,就有成百辆马车跟随,这却是我曹商超过你的地方。"

庄子说:"我听说秦王有病,召集全国的医生治疗,能够脓疮溃散疖子的人得一辆马车。舐痔疮的能得五辆马车。治病的部位越低下,得

help keep me alive?' I said to the carp, 'Carp, don't worry. I'll go to the South and persuade the king of Wu and Yue to bring the water of the Xijiang River here, and then take you to the East Sea, your hometown. Is that OK?' The carp flushed with anger, saying, 'I have lost my living environment with water, so now I have no shelter. As long as I can get a liter of water, I can survive. But you told me like that. You might as well go to the dried fish market to find me.'"

By this fable, Zhuangzi satirizes the hypocrites who are pretending generous but really mean. As the saying goes, distant water cannot quench present thirst, so don't boast and make empty talk in the way of both living and doing things.

29. Moving by Heavenly Mechanism

This fable is from "External Things", *Zhuangzi*.

Kui with one foot said to the millipede, "I have only one leg to hop along on; there's nothing better than that. Now how can you walk with so many feet?" The millipede said, "It's not like that. Don't you see the person who spits? The spittle, big as beads, small as water mist, mixed and dripping down, countless. I'm driven by the instinct heavenly mechanism to move, and I am not aware how the things work." The millipede asked the snake, "I use so many feet to walk, but not as fast as you walk with no feet. Why?" The snake said, "Action is instinctive. How can it be influenced by external things? Why would I use feet to walk?" The snake said to the wind, "I twist my back and walk on both sides as if with my feet. You are howling from the North Sea to the South, but you don't seem to use anything. How can you make that?" The wind replied, "Well, in fact you can beat me with fingers or feet, but I have no way to deal with it. While, I'm the only one who can blow the big trees and the tall buildings down. I can't deal with the small ones, but I can deal with the big ones. Only sages can defeat the great."

Zhuangzi uses this fable to show that everything has its own inherent characteristics, and each has its own advantages. If let it be, each can give play to its advantages.

30. Licking Piles for Carriages

This fable is from "Lie Yukou", *Zhuangzi*.

There was a man named Cao Shang in the state of Song. The king of Song

的马车越多。你难道舔了他的痔疮了吗？要不怎么能获得那么多的马车呢？你还是快走开吧！"

庄子借这则寓言讽刺了那些为了发家致富而不择手段、趋炎附势的人。这里，庄子没有给曹商留情面，从此，曹商也因"舐痔得车"而臭名远扬。一个人拥有财富的多少，并不能说明其人格的高下。说不定那些使他自以为荣耀无比的财富，正是它低下人格的标志呢。

31. 大小之别

这则寓言出自《庄子·逍遥游》。

有一本书叫《齐谐》，专门记载怪异的事，书中说："鸟迁徙到南方的大海，翅膀拍击水面，激起波涛三千里，盘旋而上直冲九万里的高空，它起飞后，六个月才停息下来。"这是大鹏在空中往下看的样子。

再说水积不深，则没有浮力负载大船。但倒杯水在厅堂低洼处，芥草也可以当作船。

风聚积的力量不雄厚，大鹏的翅膀就托不起来。所以，大鹏高飞九万里，要有风在下面托着。大鹏凭借风力，才能背负青天，没有阻挡地飞到南方去。

知了和斑鸠嘲笑大鹏说："我们什么时候愿意起飞就飞起来，碰到榆树或檀树，就停在那上面，没有力气了就落在地面上，为什么要飞到九万里的高空向南飞去呢？"到附近苍茫的野外去，只需带三顿饭就够了；到百里之外去，要用一宿的时间准备干粮；到千里之外去，就得用三个月时间准备干粮。

《齐谐》这本书最后说：小小的知了、斑鸠懂得什么呢！

这则寓言常用来比喻各人境界大小有差别，境界小者体会不到境界大者的深邃思想。一个人若不能提升自己的思想境界，就只能满足于现状，碌碌无为。

sent him to the state of Qin. When Cao set out, the king of Song gave him several carriages. When he arrived in the state of Qin, the king of Qin appreciated him and gave him a hundred carriages.

After returning to the state of Song, Cao saw Zhuangzi and showed off to him, "Living in poor alleyways and cramped lanes, skimping, starving, weaving straw sandals for a living. That's where I'm not as good as you. Once getting the chance to meet the King, I have hundreds of carriages follow me. This is the place where I can surpass you."

Zhuangzi said, "I heard that the king of Qin was ill. He called doctors all over the country to treat him. Those who were able to cure the abscess would get a carriage. He who licks piles gets five carriages. The lower the site of treatment, the more carriages will be given. Did you lick his piles? How else can you get so many carriages? You'd better go at once."

By this fable, Zhuangzi satirizes those people who try every fair means to get rich. Here, Zhuangzi didn't spare Cao Shang's feeling. From then on, Cao Shang was also notorious for "licking piles for carriages". The amount of wealth a person has does not mean the height of his personality. Maybe the wealth that made him proud was the mark of his petty personality.

31. Differences Between Great and Small

This fable is from "Wandering in Absolute Freedom", *Zhuangzi*.

There is a book called *Qixie*, a collection of mysterious stories. It is said in the book, "When the bird was removing to the southern sea, its wings stirred up waves for 3000 Li. By a strong whirlwind, it was soaring to 90 thousand Li for half a year, and then stopped." This is how the bird Peng looks like down in the air.

Besides, if the water is not deep, there will be no buoyancy to load the ship. But pour a glass of water in the low-lying part of the hall; mustard can also be used as a boat.

The strength of wind accumulation is not strong; the wings of Peng cannot hold up. Therefore, there must be wind under to uphold the Peng to fly 90000 Li. With the help of the wind, the Peng can fly to the south against the sky without obstruction.

32. 不龟手之药

这则寓言出自《庄子·逍遥游》。龟手，冻裂手上的皮肤。

宋国有个人善于炮制防止冻裂的不龟手之药，他的家族世世代代以漂洗丝绵为职业，始终勤勤恳恳，但由于收入菲薄，生活总是很贫困。

有个外地人，听说有不龟手之药的秘方，愿以百金求购。这可是个大数目！不龟手之药的主人动心了。但想到祖传的秘方要卖出去，也是件大事，于是集合全家族的成员共商转让之事。大家七嘴八舌一番议论，最后总算统一了思想：祖祖辈辈以漂洗丝絮为生，收入太少，今天一旦出售药方，可以获取大笔金钱，何乐而不为？于是全体成员一致同意把药方卖出去。

客人得到秘方以后，立即奔赴吴国，对吴王说，今后将士在寒冬打仗，再也不用为冻手犯难了。不久，越国大军压境，吴国告急，吴王委任此人统帅大军。此时正值严冬，吴越两军又是进行水战。由于吴军将士涂抹了不龟手之药，战斗力特别旺盛，因而大胜越军。班师回朝后，吴王大喜过望，颁诏犒赏三军，同时将献药之人视为有特殊贡献的统帅，割地封赏嘉奖他。

这则寓言告诉我们，同样一个事物，由于使用方法和对象不同，其结果和收效也会大不一样。

The cicada and turtledove laughed at the Peng and said, "When we want to take off, we will fly. When we meet elms or sandalwood trees, we will stop there. If we are tired, we will land on the ground. Why do we want to fly to an altitude of 90000 Li and fly south?" If we go off to the green woods nearby, we just need to take along food for three meals; If we go a hundred miles away, we need to spend a night preparing solid food; To go thousands of miles away, it will take three months to prepare the food.

It is written in the end of *Qixie*, How can the little cicada and turtledove know the ambition of the Peng!

This fable is often used to describe the difference of people's realm, great or small, and the small one can't understand the profound thought of the big one. If one can't improve one's ideological realm, one can only be satisfied with the status quo without great accomplishment.

32. A Salve to Prevent Chapped Hands

This fable is from "Wandering in Absolute Freedom", *Zhuangzi*. Chapped hands mean frostbite skin on hands.

There was a man in the state of Song who was good at making salves to prevent chapped hands. His family took washing silk floss as their profession from generation to generation and were always diligent. However, because of poor income, they always lived in poverty.

A stranger had heard that there was a secret recipe for this medicine. He was willing to buy it with 100 gold. That's a lot of money for the poor family. So, the owner of the salve to prevent chapped hands was moved. But it was also a big deal to think of selling the secret recipe handed down by ancestors, so he gathered members of the whole family to discuss the transfer. After discussion about the case with different opinions, it finally came to an agreement that, "We have been washing silk floss for generations, and the income is too small. Now once we sell the prescriptions, we can get a lot of money. Why not?" So all the members of the family agreed to sell the prescription.

After the stranger got the secret recipe, he immediately went to the state of Wu and told the king that in the future, soldiers would fight in the cold winter without worrying about the crapped hands. Soon after, the Yue army came down

33. 许由辞帝位

这则寓言出自《庄子·逍遥游》。

古代有个帝王，名字叫尧。尧打算把天下让给许由，说："太阳和月亮都已升起来了，这时还在点燃火炬，要它跟太阳和月亮比光亮，不是很难吗？季雨及时降落了，可是还在不停地浇水灌地，对于润泽农作物来说，不显得徒劳吗？先生如能为天下之主，天下一定会获得大治。可是我还空居其位，我自己感到很羞愧，请允许我把天下交给你。"

许由回答说："你治理天下，天下已经获得了大治，而我却还要去替代你，我是为了名声吗？'名'是'实'所派生出来的次要东西，我怎么会去追求这次要的东西呢？鹪鹩在森林中筑巢，不过占用一棵树枝；鼹鼠到大河边饮水，不过喝满肚子。你还是打消念头回去吧，天下对于我来说没有什么用处啊！厨师即使不下厨，祭祀主持人也不会越俎代庖的！"

庄子借这则寓言表达了自己主张自然无为，无功无名的人生追求，对功名利禄的淡泊和超脱，对统治阶级的蔑视。

to the border of Wu. In such an emergent situation, the King of Wu appointed this man to command the army. It was a severe winter, and the Wu and Yue armies were engaged in water war again. Because the soldiers of Wu army smeared the salve to prevent chapped hands, their combat effectiveness was very strong, so they won a great victory over the Yue army. After they returned to the court, the king of Wu was overjoyed and issued an imperial edict to reward the army. At the same time, he regarded the man who offered the medicine as the commander with special contributions and gave him a special reward.

This fable tells us that the same thing, due to different usages and objects of use, will have different results and effects.

33. Xu You Resigning the Throne

This fable is from "Wandering in Absolute Freedom", *Zhuangzi*.

In ancient times, there was an emperor named Yao. Yao intended to resign the throne to Xu You, "Isn't it a waste of light if the torch is still burning when the sun and the moon have already come out? Isn't it a waste of labor if one continues to water the fields when timely rains have been falling? If you can be the master of the world, the world will be surely in great order. But I am still on the throne, so I feel very ashamed. Please allow me to resign the throne to you."

Xu You replied, "Since you govern the country, it has been in good order. If I were to take your place, would I be seeking after name?" A name is but the shadow of reality, and should I pursue such a shadow? The wren that builds a nest in the deep forest occupies only a single branch likewise the mole that drinks from the river takes only a bellyful. You'd better give up the idea and go back. The throne is useless to me! Even if the chef is not cooking, the priest in charge of the offering ceremony should not come to the kitchen to take the place of his duty."

By this fable, Zhuangzi expresses his pursuit of natural inaction, futility and anonymity, his indifference to fame and wealth, and his contempt for the ruling class.

34. 大瓠无用

这则寓言出自《庄子·逍遥游》。

惠子对庄子说:"魏王送我大葫芦种子,我把它培植后,结出的果实有五石容量。用大葫芦去盛水,但是它的坚固程度却承受不了水的压力。把它剖开做瓢也太大了,没有那么大的水缸可以放得下。这个葫芦太大了,我因为它大而无用就把它砸烂了。"

庄子说:"先生您实在是不善于使用大东西啊!如今你有五石容积的大葫芦,为什么不考虑用它来制成腰舟,而浮游于江湖之上,却担忧葫芦太大无处可容呢?看来先生你还是心窍不通啊!"

庄子借这则寓言告诫人们,无用与有用是相对的,看似无用的东西,实则有大用,关键是看你怎么用。

35. 秦失吊丧

这则寓言出自《庄子·养生主》。

老聃死了,他的朋友秦失去吊丧,大哭几声便离开了。老聃的弟子问道:"你不是我们老师生前的好友吗?"秦失说:"是的。"弟子们又问:"那么吊唁朋友像这样,行吗?"秦失说:"行。原来我认为你们跟随老师多年都是超然物外的人了,现在看来并不是这样的。刚才我进入灵房去吊唁,看见有老年人在哭,好像做父母的哭自己的孩子;有年轻人在哭,好像做孩子的哭自己的父母。他们之所以会聚在这里痛哭,一定有不想吊唁而吊唁,有不想哭泣而哭泣的。这是违反常理、背弃真情的。你们都忘掉了人是秉承于自然、受命于天的道理,古时候称这种做法为背离自然的过失。偶然来到世上,你们的老师他应时而生;离开人世,你们的老师他顺应自然而死。如果安于天理和常分,顺从自然和变化,那么哀乐之情便都不能进入心怀。古时候人们称这样做就叫自然的解脱。"

庄子借这则寓言告诫世人,人的死亡是回归自然,所以要正确对待

34. A Huge Gourd of No Use

The fable is from "Wandering in Absolute Freedom", *Zhuangzi*.

Huizi said to Zhuangzi, "The king of Wei sent me seeds of huge gourd. After I planted them, the fruit can hold five piculs. I tried using it as a water container, but it was so heavy that I couldn't lift it. I split it in half to make dippers, but they were so huge that I couldn't keep them in water tanks. This gourd is too huge. I broke it because it was too big to use."

Zhuangzi said, "Sir, you are not good at using big things! Now you, Sir, have such a huge guard which can hold five piculs, why don't you think of making a boat with it by means of which you could have floated over rivers and lakes, but worry about the gourd is too big to be kept? It seems that sir, your mind is not open enough yet!"

Zhuangzi uses this fable to warn people that uselessness is relative to usefulness. What seems to be useless is of great use. The key is the way of using.

35. Qin Shi Mourning for Laozi

This fable is from "Essentials for Keeping Good Health", *Zhuangzi* .

Laozi died, and his friend Qin Shi came to mourn him. Qin cried a few times and left. Laozi's disciples asked, "Aren't you our master's best friend?" Qin Shi said, "Yes." The disciples asked again, "Well, how can you mourn for friends like this?" Qin Shi said, "Well, I have thought that you have been detached from things since you have followed your master for many years. Now it doesn't seem that way. Just now when I went into the mourning room, I saw some old people crying, like parents crying for their children; There are young people crying, like children crying for their parents. They are gathering here to wail, but there must be some people who mourn and wail not out of their true feelings. This is against common sense and betrays the true feeling. You all forget that man is born of nature and given birth by heaven. Such mourning or crying was taken as a mistake to deviate from nature in ancient times. Your master happened to come because it was the proper time for his born; he happened to leave because it was the simple sequence of the nature by which your master should die. If one is content with whatever happens at the right time and follow the natural course, sorrow and joy will not affect him. This is what the ancients called 'free from bondage'."

死亡。同时也揭露了他人之哭并非出于真情。

36. 支离疏养生

这则寓言出自《庄子·人间世》。支离疏，形体不全的人。

支离疏的下巴隐藏在肚脐下，双肩高于头顶，后脑下的发髻指向天空，五官的出口也都向上，两条大腿和两边的胸肋并生在一起。他给人缝衣浆洗，足够糊口度日；又替人筛糠簸米，足可养活十口人。政府征兵时，支离疏却捋袖扬臂在征兵人面前游逛。国君有大的差役，支离疏却因身有残疾而免除劳役。国君向残疾人赈济粮食，支离疏还能领得三钟米和十捆柴草。像支离疏那样形体残缺不全的人，还能够养活自己，终享天年，又何况一个身体健全的人呢！

庄子借这则寓言意在说明无用与有用之间的辩证关系，一个人因身体残缺，对社会无用，但在动荡的社会里，却因无用于社会而终养天年。

37. 无趾务学

这则寓言出自《庄子·德充符》。

鲁国有个被砍去脚趾的人叫叔山无趾，他用脚跟走路去见孔子，希望能做孔子的学生。孔子打量了一番，说："你从前不懂规矩，犯有前科，遭受惩罚变成了现在这副样子。已经太晚了，怎么来得及补救呢！"

无趾说："那时候我幼稚不懂事，自轻自贱，为非作歹，被人砍掉了一只脚。现在来到这里，但我身上还有比脚更尊贵的东西，我要使他保存完美。天是没有什么不覆盖的，地是没有什么不承载的。我把先生看作无不负载的天地，哪里知道先生是这样的人呢！"

孔子回过头来，对无趾说："我的修养浅陋，不敢妄比天地。但我想请先生谈谈天地之间的大道。"

Zhuangzi uses this fable to warn people that death is a return to nature, so we should treat death correctly. At the same time, it also reveals that other people's crying is not out of their true feelings.

36. Zhili Shu Preserving Health

This fable is from "Ways of the Human World", *Zhuangzi*. Zhili Shu, a man with a distorted body.

His chin was stuck down under the naval; his shoulders were higher than the head; his bun on the back of the head pointed to the sky; his nostrils, eyes and mouth are all pointed upward; his thighs were pressed to his ribs. He made a living by sewing, washing and starching for others; he could also feed his family with dozens of people by sifting chaff and winnowing rice for others. When the government conscripted, he was wandering in front of the recruiters waving goodbye; when there was big forced labor, he would be excused, because of his disability. On the other hand, when the government donated grain to the disabled, Zhili Shu could receive rice as much as three cups and ten faggots of firewood. A person with crippled body like Zhili Shu can support himself and enjoy his life, not to mention a healthy person!

Zhuangzi uses this fable to illustrate the dialectical relationship between uselessness and usefulness. A person is useless to the society because of his disabled body, but in a turbulent society, such a useless person can enjoy his life span just because he is useless.

37. Wuzhi Striving to Learn

This fable is from "Signs of Complete Virtue", *Zhuangzi*.

There was a man in the state of Lu who had his toes cut off, called Shushan Wuzhi (Wuzhi means no toes). He walked with his heels to visit Confucius, hoping to be a student of him. Confucius looked at him and said, "You used to be unruly, guilty and punished like this. It's too late. How can you remedy it by learning from me?"

Wuzhi said, "At that time, I was childish and self-contemptuous, so I was cut off one foot for doing evil. Now I'm here, because there's something more valuable than feet, and I want to make it complete and perfect. There is nothing not

无趾转身走了。孔子对弟子们说:"你们自己要努力啊!叔山无趾是个被别人砍断脚趾的人,还在致力求学以弥补过去品行上的污点,何况你们这些品行上并没有污点的人呢!"

庄子借这则寓言告诫人们,一个人如果有了污点,应该正视自己的污点,勇于改过,找到属于自己的人生道路。

38. 子桑思贫

这则寓言出自《庄子·大宗师》。

子舆和子桑是好朋友。连绵的大雨下了十天,子舆说:"子桑恐怕已经饿倒了吧。"于是便包着饭菜前去给子桑吃。来到子桑门前,就听见子桑好像在唱歌,又像在哭泣,并且还弹着琴:"父亲啊!母亲啊!苍天啊!大地啊!人们啊!"歌声很微弱,急促地吐露着歌词。

子舆走进屋子,问道:"你歌唱的诗词为什么是这种调子?"

子桑回答说:"我正在探寻使我达到如此贫困地步的原因,然而没有找到。父母难道会希望我贫困吗?苍天没有偏私地覆盖着整个大地,大地没有偏私地负载着所有生灵,天地怎么会偏私不公地让我贫困呢?我在寻找使我贫困的原因,可是我没能找到。既然这样,那么让我达到如此这般地步,还是'命'啊!"

子桑认为造成自己贫穷的原因是"命",这显然是一种宿命论的观点。拥有这种观点的人,常常不思进取,安于现状,悲观消极。面对困境,只有积极进取,寻找解决困难的办法,方是良策。

covered by the sky and nothing not carried by the earth. I regard you my master as Heaven and Earth. But how can I know that you are not such a person?"

Confucius looked back and said to Wuzhi, "My cultivation is so shallow that I dare not compare with Heaven and Earth. But I'd like to ask you to talk about the way between Heaven and Earth."

Wuzhi turned and left. Confucius said to his disciples, "You have to work hard! Shushan Wuzhi is a man whose toes have been cut off, but he is still studying hard to make up for the blemish in his past conduct, not to mention you guys who have no blemish in your conduct."

Zhuangzi uses this fable to warn people that if a person has a stain, he should face up to his stain, have the courage to change his mistakes and find his own way of life.

38. Zisang Contemplating Poverty

This fable is from "Great and Venerable Master", *Zhuangzi*.

Ziyu and Zisang were good friends. After ten days of continuous heavy rain, Ziyu talked to himself, "I'm afraid Zisang is hungry to fall in a faint." So he packed the food and went to Zisang's house. When he came to Zisang's door, he heard that Zisang was singing, or crying and playing the instrument, "Oh, my father! Oh, my mother! Oh, my God! The earth! The men!" The voice of the song was very weak, and the words were spewed out in a hurry.

Ziyu entered the room and asked, "Why is the tune of your songs like that?"

Zisang replied, "I'm looking for the reasons why I'm so poor, but I can't find them. Would my parents have wished me to be so poor? The heaven is no partial to cover the whole earth, and the earth was in the same way to carry all the creatures. How can Heaven and Earth make me poor? I'm looking for the cause of my poverty, but in vain. In this case, it's still fate which makes me reach such a state!"

Zisang thinks that the cause of his poverty is "fate", which is obviously a fatalistic view. People with this view are often not enterprising, content with the status quo, pessimistic and negative. In the face of difficulties, it is only a good strategy to make positive progress and find solutions.

39. 盗也有道

这则寓言出自《庄子·胠箧》。

强盗首领盗跖的部下问盗跖说:"做大盗也有法则吗?"盗跖回答说:"无论做什么事情,都有法则可言。如果凭空能猜出屋里储藏着多少财物,这就是圣明;如果能带头先进入屋里抢东西,这就是勇敢;如果是最后退出屋子,就是义气;判断能否动手,这就是智慧;如果分赃均匀,这就是仁德。不具备这五种素质而成为大盗,是不可能的。"

庄子借这则寓言说明了"道"无处不在,即使做强盗,也有"法则"可遵循。当然,庄子借这则寓言告诫世人,人做坏事,常常会把话说得冠冕堂皇,我们不能被这些假象所迷惑。

40. 吕梁丈夫

这则寓言出自《庄子·达生》。

孔子在吕梁瀑布边游览,看见瀑布有三千丈高,浪花溅出四十里,鼋、鼍、鱼、鳖都不能游过去,却看见一个男人在水里游泳。孔子以为他是因痛苦而想自杀的人,便叫弟子们顺着水流去救他。谁知这个人游了几百步,从激流中钻出来了,披着头发唱着歌,在堤岸上漫步。

孔子连忙赶上去问他:"我还以为你是水中的鬼怪,但仔细看,原来你是人。请问你游泳有什么秘诀吗?"

那人说:"没有,我没有什么秘诀。我从固有开始而安于环境,由着天性生长而养成习惯,顺着命运安排而听任自然,和漩涡一起进入水流的中心,与涌出的流水一起浮出水面,顺从水的流动方向而不另出己见。这就是我能在水里游来游去的缘故啊。"

孔子又问:"什么叫安于环境、养成习惯、听任自然呢?"

那人说:"我生在山里就安心住在山上,这就是安于环境;我从小长在水边就安心住在水边,在水中浮游直到长大,就安于浮水,这就叫作养成习惯。我不知道为什么会成功却成功了,这就是顺其自然。"

39. Tao of Robbers

This fable is from "Break Open the Boxes", *Zhuangzi*.

Robber Zhi was a bandit leader. One day his subordinate asked him, "Is there a Tao to be a robber?" Robber Zhi replied, "Whatever you do, there are rules. If you can guess out how much property is stored in the house based on nothing, it is pure intellect. If you can take the lead in robbing things in the house, that's courage; If you are the last to leave the house, it's loyalty; It's wisdom to judge whether we can do it or not; If the spoils are evenly distributed, this is benevolence. It is impossible to be a robber without these five qualities."

Zhuangzi uses this fable to show that "Tao" is everywhere. Even the robbers should follow "rules". Of course, Zhuangzi uses this fable to warn the world that when people do bad things, they often speak with high sounding words, so we should not be confused by these illusions.

40. A Man at Lvliang

This fable is from "Full Understanding of Life", *Zhuangzi*.

When Confucius visited the Lvliang waterfall, he saw that the waterfall was 3000 feet high, and the spray splashed out for 40 Li. Even the tortoise, alligator, fish and turtle could not swim there, but he saw a man swimming in the water. Confucius thought that he was a man who was committing suicide because of pain, so he asked his disciples to follow the current to save him. Unexpectedly this man swam hundreds of steps, got out of the torrent, dressed in hair, sang songs, and walked on the bank.

Confucius rushed to ask him, "I thought you were a ghost in the water, but look at you carefully, you are human. Do you have any tips for swimming?"

The man said, "No, I don't have any secret. I start from the inherent and be content with the environment, grow up by nature and form habits. Following the fate and let it be, I dive in the water with whirlpool in the very center of its whirl, and come up again with it when it whirls the other way. I follow the way of the water, and do nothing contrary to it. That's why I can swim around in the water."

Confucius asked again, "What does it mean to be content with the environment, to form habits and to let nature take its course?"

The man said, "Since I was born in the mountains, I was content to live in the

这则寓言告诫人们，只有经历长期实践，才能掌握自然规律，做到顺其自然。

41. 云将东游

这则寓言出自《庄子·在宥》。

云将到东方去巡游，经过神木扶摇的枝旁恰巧遇上了鸿蒙。鸿蒙正拍着大腿像雀儿一样跳跃游乐。云将见鸿蒙这般模样，惊讶地停下来，纹丝不动地站着，说："老先生是什么人啊！您为什么要这样做呢？"鸿蒙拍着大腿不停地跳跃，对云将说："自在地游乐！"云将说："我想向你请教。"鸿蒙抬起头来看了看云将道："哎！"

云将说："天上之气不和谐，地上之气郁结了，阴、阳、风、雨、晦、明六气不调和，四时变化不合节令。如今我希望调谐六气之精华来养育众生，对此将怎么办？"鸿蒙拍着大腿掉过头去，说："我不知道！我不知道！"云将得不到回答。

过了三年，云将又到东方去巡游。经过宋国境界的时候，恰巧又遇上了鸿蒙。云将大喜，快步来靠近鸿蒙说："你老先生忘记了我吗？你老先生忘记了我吗？"叩头至地行了大礼，希望得到鸿蒙的指教。鸿蒙说："自由自在地去游玩，不知道追求什么。漫不经心地随意活动，不知道往哪里去。游人纷纷攘攘，观赏那虚无的情景；我又能知道什么！"云将说："我自以为能够随心地活动，人民也都跟着我走；我不得已而对人民有所亲近，如今却为人民所效仿。我希望能聆听您的教诲。"鸿蒙说："扰乱自然的常规，违背事物的真情，整个自然的变化不能顺应形成。离散群居的野兽，飞翔的鸟儿都夜鸣，灾害波及草木，祸患波及昆虫。唉，这都是治理天下的过错！"云将问："那么我将怎么办呢？"鸿蒙说："唉，你受到的毒害实在太深了！你还是就这么回去吧。"云将说："我遇见你实在不容易，恳切希望能听到你的指教。"鸿蒙说："唉！修身养性。你只要处心于无为之境，万物会自然

mountains, which is to be content with the environment; Since I grew up at the water's edge, I have lived at the water's edge with ease. I float in the water until I grow up. This is called forming a habit. I don't know why I succeed, but I succeed. That's let it be."

This fable tells us that only through long-term practice can we master the laws of nature and let it be.

41. Yunjiang Traveling to the East

The fable is from "Let Be and Let Alone", *Zhuangzi*.

When Yunjiang was going eastwards, he passed through the branches of Fuyao (a magic tree) and happened to meet Hongmeng (Natural Energy). Hongmeng is patting his thighs and jumping like a sparrow. Yunjiang stopped in surprise by seeing such a scene, stood still and said, "Who are you, senior gentleman? And why are you doing so?" Beating his thighs and jumping, Hongmeng relpied, "I am just playing freely! " Yunjiang said, "I want to consult you." Hungmeng looked up at Yunjiang and said, "Well."

Yunjiang continued, "The breath of heaven is out of Harmony; the breath of earth is at a standstill; the six elemental influences, including Yin, Yang, Wind, Rain, Obscurity and Brightness do not act in concord; the four seasons do not observe their proper times. Now I wish to blend together the essence of the six influences in order to nourish all living things, so what should I do about this?" Hongmeng patted his thigh, turned his head and said, "I don't know! I don't know! " So, Yunjiang got no answers.

After three years, Yunjiang traveled to the east again. When he was passing by the state of Song on his way, he happened to meet Hongmeng again. Yunjiang was overjoyed and dashed forward, saying, "Have you forgotten me, my senior gentleman? Have you forgotten me, my senior gentleman?" He kowtowed to the ground, hoping to beg for instructions from Hongmeng. Hongmeng said, "I don't know what to pursue, and just play freely. I don't know where to go. There are so many tourists, watching the scene of nothingness; What can I know!"Yunjiang said, "I thought I could do whatever I wanted, and the people followed me; I had to be close to the people, but now I am followed by the people. I hope to hear from your advice and instruction." Hongmeng said, "It disturbs the conventions of

地有所变化。忘却你的形体，废弃你的智慧，让伦理和万物一块儿遗忘。混同于茫茫的自然之气，解除思虑释放精神，像死灰一样木然地没有魂灵。万物纷杂繁多，全都各自回归本性，各自回归本性却是出自无心，浑然无知保持本真，终身不得背违；假如有所感知，就是背离本真。不要询问它们的名称，不要窥测它们的实情，万物本是自然地生长。"云将说："你把对待外物和对待自我的要领传授给我，你把清心寂神的方法晓谕给我；我亲身探求大道，如今方才有所领悟。"叩头至地再次行了大礼，起身告别而去。

这则寓言告诉我们，万事万物都有自身规律，只有顺从规律，才能把事情做好。如果违背常规而主观臆断，就会失败。

42. 削木为镰

这则寓言出自《庄子·达生》。

梓庆是一名出色的木匠，他拥有一门绝技，能把木头削刻成一种名叫镰的乐器。镰做成以后，看见的人无不为之惊叹，认为是鬼斧神工。

鲁侯听说了，就召见了梓庆，问道："梓庆，你用什么办法做成这么好的镰啊？"

梓庆回答道："我只是个工匠，没有什么特别高明的技术！虽说如此，不过，我还是有一种本事。我在准备做镰时，从不敢随便耗费精神，必定斋戒来静养心思。斋戒三天，我就会忘记做成之后的庆贺、赏赐，因而就不会有获取功名利禄的想法。斋戒五天，不再心存非议、夸誉、技巧或笨拙的杂念，就不会在乎别人的评价了。斋戒七天，已不为外物所动，仿佛忘掉了自己的四肢和形体，忘掉了外界的一切纷扰，心里只是想着怎么能做好镰了。斋戒过后，我便进入山林，仔细观察各种木料的质地；谨慎地选择外形与体态最与镰相合的材料，直到心里有了镰的样子，然后才开始动手加工制作。如果不是这样，我就停止不做。这就是用我木工的纯真本性融合木料的自然天性，制成的器物疑为鬼斧

nature, violates the true nature of things, and prevents the accomplishment of the natural changes. Instead, the beasts are scattered from their herds; the birds are crying all night; disaster is coming to the grass and trees; destruction is reaching to the insects. Alas, it's all the fault of governing the state!" Yunjiang asked, "And what shall I do?" Hongmeng said, "Well, you are so deeply poisoned! You'd better go back." Yunjiang said, "It's not easy for me to meet you, and I sincerely beg for your instructions." Hongmeng said, "Well, do you know about self-cultivation? As long as you rest in inaction, everything will transform naturally by themselves. Forget your body, discard your wisdom, let ethics and all things be forgotten together. You only have to mingle yourself with the essence of nature, free yourself of worries and cares, and become as soulless as dead ashes. And then, the ten thousand things one by one will return to the root without knowing why. Dark and undifferentiated to keep their own nature, none will depart from it to the end of life. But if you try to know it, you have already departed from the inborn nature. Don't ask for their names; don't pry into their truth; everything grows naturally." Yunjiang said, "You taught me the essentials of treating external things and myself, the method of purifying the mind and calming the spirit; I've been exploring the Tao, and now I begin to understand it." He kowtowed to the ground again and got up to say goodbye.

This fable tells us that everything has its own natural law, and only by obeying the natural law can we do things well. If we go against the laws and make subjective assumptions, we will fail.

42. Carving Wood into Ju

This fable is from "Full Understanding of Life", *Zhuangzi*.

Ziqing was an excellent carpenter, who had a unique skill to carve wood into a kind of musical instrument called Ju. After Ju was made, all the people who saw it marveled at it and praised it uncanny workmanship.

When Marquis Lu heard this, he summoned Ziqing and asked, "Ziqing the Carpenter, how can you make it so marvelous?"

Ziqing replied, "I'm nothing more than a craftsman. I don't have any special skills! But there is one thing I need to tell you. When I am about to do it, I never dare to distract my energy. I must fast to cultivate and compose my mind and

神工的原因吧!"

这则寓言告诫我们,要做好一件事,必须专心致志,排除外界干扰。

43. 桓公见鬼

这则寓言出自《庄子·达生》。

有一次,齐桓公在沼泽地里打猎,管仲亲自为齐桓公驾车。突然间,齐桓公看见了鬼。齐桓公赶紧握着管仲的手,惊魂未定地问:"仲父,你看到什么了吗?"

管仲回答:"我什么也没有看到。"

齐桓公打猎回宫以后,因受到惊吓与疲惫困倦,从此就病倒了,好几天卧床不起。这时,有个名叫皇子告敖的读书人主动求见齐桓公,对他说:"这是您自己伤害了自己,鬼怎么能伤害得了您呢?一个人的体内如果产生了怒气并且郁结起来,那么他的精魂就会游离于体外而使人精神恍惚,对于来自外界的骚扰也就缺乏足够的精神力量;郁结着的气上升而不下降,人就会容易发脾气;郁结着的气下降而不上升,就会使人健忘;而如果这股郁结着的气不上不下,恰好郁结在身体的正中而不离散,人就会生病。"

齐桓公听后,半信半疑地问道:"那么,世上到底有没有鬼呢?"

皇子告敖肯定地回答:"有!水中污泥里有叫履的鬼,灶房里有叫髻的鬼。门户内的各种烦攘,有个叫雷霆的鬼住在那里;东北的墙脚下,时常有名叫倍阿鲑蠪的鬼出没其间;西北方的墙脚下,名叫攻入阳的鬼住在那里。水里有水鬼罔象,丘陵里有山鬼峷,大山里有山鬼夔,郊野里有野鬼彷徨,草泽里还有一种名叫委蛇的鬼。"

齐桓公听了,赶紧追问:"请问,委蛇的形状是什么样子?"

皇子告敖形容说:"委蛇嘛,身躯像车毂那么大,像车辕那么长,穿着紫衣裳,戴着红帽子。作为鬼神,委蛇特别不喜欢雷车发出的隆隆

spirit. Fasting for three days, I no longer have the idea of celebrations and rewards for my work, and the idea of gaining fame and fortune. Fasting for five days, I no longer have distracting thoughts of criticism, praise, skill or clumsiness, and care about other's evaluation. After fasting for seven days, I will not move by external things. It seemed that I have forgotten my limbs and body, and all the troubles of the external world. What I am keen on is how to make Ju well. After fasting, I will go into the mountains and carefully observe the texture of all kinds of wood; carefully choose the wood with the most consistent appearance and posture with Ju. Only when there was the form of Ju in my heart can I begin to make it. If I can't find such perfect wood or have no idea of the form of Ju in my mind, I'll stop. This is the reason why the instrument, made from mingling my pure nature of woodworking and the nature of wood, is suspected to be uncanny craftsmanship!"

This fable tells us that if we want to do a good job, we must concentrate on it and eliminate external interference.

43. Duke Huan Seeing the Ghost

This fable is from "Full Understanding of Life", *Zhuangzi*.

Once, Duke Huan of Qi was hunting in the swamp, and Guan Zhong himself drove for him. Suddenly, Duke Huan saw a ghost. He quickly grasped Guan Zhong's hand and asked in shock, "Zhong, did you see anything?"

Guan Zhong replied, "No, I didn't."

After returning to the palace from hunting, Duke Huan was frightened and tired, so he fell ill and was bedridden for several days. At this time, a scholar named Huangzi Gao'ao begged for meeting Duke Huan and told him, "It is you that hurt yourself. How can a ghost hurt you? If there is anger and depression standing still in one's body, then his spirit will detach from his body and fall in a trance, and he will be troubled by the external harassment because the lack of concentrated spirit; If the stagnant breath of anger rises but does not fall, people will lose their temper easily; If the stagnant breath falls but does not rise, it will make people forgetful; And if this stagnant breath is not up and down, but it happens to be stagnant in the middle of the body and stands still, people will get sick."

声响,一听到这种声音就会双手抱头而立。谁如果能见到委蛇,这个人恐怕将要成为霸主了!"

齐桓公听了这一席话,顿时开怀大笑。他兴奋地说:"我所见到的鬼,正是你说的这种委蛇啊!"于是,他赶紧整理好衣冠,与皇子告敖坐着交谈。不到一天的时间,齐桓公的病就不知不觉地好了。

这则寓言说明了,一个人如果精神恍惚,无病也会被折磨成有病。如果精神愉快,心情畅达,病魔就会远离。

44. 老汉粘蝉

这则寓言出自《庄子·达生》。

孔子带着弟子到楚国去,路上经过一个树林,看见树林中有个驼背老人正在用竹竿粘蝉。老人粘蝉非常轻松熟练,就像在地上捡取蝉一样。

孔子问:"先生的动作真是巧啊!有什么门道吗?"

老人说:"我确实有我自己的办法。我经过了五六个月的练习,在竿头累叠起两个丸子而不会坠落,这样失手的情况已经很少了;叠起三个丸子而不坠落,这样失手的情况十次也不会超过一次;叠起五个丸子而不坠落,就会像在地上拾取蝉一样容易了。我立定身子,犹如临近地面的断木桩,我举竿的手臂就像枯木的树枝。虽然天地很大,万物品类繁多,但我一心只专注于蝉的翅膀,从不思前想后、左顾右盼,绝不因纷繁的万物而改变对蝉翼的注意,这样做,怎么能不成功呢?"

孔子听了,转过身来对弟子们说:"专心致志不分散注意力,就是高度凝聚精神,本领就可以练到出神入化的地步。这恐怕就是驼背老人所说的道理。"

这则寓言说明了,一个人如果能够专心致志,勤学苦练,就能把本领练到出神入化的地步。

After hearing this, Duke Huan asked suspiciously, "So, is there ghost in the world?"

Huangzi Gao'ao definitely answered, "Yes! There is a ghost named Lu in the mud of water, and a ghost named Ji in the kitchen. There are all kinds of troubles in the family due to a ghost named Leiting (thunder) who lives there; At the northeast corner of the wall, the ghost named Beia Guilong often leaps about; And the northwest corner is where the ghost named Yiyang lives. There is the water ghost (Wangxiang) in the water, the hill ghost (Shen) in the hills, the mountain ghost (Kui) in the mountains, the wild ghost (the Panghuang) wandering in the countryside, and a ghost named Weishe in the grass."

On hearing this, Duke Huan immediately continued to ask, "Excuse me, what's the shape of the Weishe?"

Huangzi Gao'ao said,"Weishe is as big as a hub and as long as a shaft, wearing purple clothes and a red hat. As a ghost, Weishe doesn't like the rumble of the thunder. When he hears the sound, he will hold his head in his hands. If anyone can see Weishe, I'm afraid he will become the King!"

Hearing this, Duke Huan bursted into laughter. He said excitedly, "The ghost I saw is exactly Weishe that you said!" Therefore, he hastened to tidy up his clothes and sat talking with Huangzi Gao'ao.In less than one day, Duke Huan recovered unconsciously.

This fable shows that if one is in a trance, he will be tortured to be sick even though he is physically healthy. If one can keep a happy spirit and smooth mood, he will be forever far away from the trouble of disease.

44. An Old Man Sticking Cicadas

This fable is from "Full Understanding of Life", *Zhuangzi*.

Confucius took his disciples to the state of Chu. On the way through a forest, he saw an old man with a hunchback sticking cicadas by a bamboo pole. The old man sticks cicadas very easily and skillfully, just like picking cicadas on the ground.

Confucius asked, "How skillful you are, sir! Is there any knack?"

The old man said, "I do have my own way. After five or six months of practice, I have piled up two balls at the end of the pole without falling, so that there are

45. 举鲁儒服

这则寓言出自《庄子·田子方》。

庄子拜见鲁哀公，鲁哀公告诉他："现在鲁国儒家学派的学者多，先生这一学派的人少。"庄子听了，回答说："鲁国儒家的学者少。"哀公听了感觉很奇怪，就说："整个鲁国的人都穿着儒服，怎么能够说少呢？"庄子回答说："我听说，儒家学者戴圆顶帽子的，懂得天时变化。穿方鞋的人，了解地形情况。用五色丝带系玉玦的，遇事能够决断。我认为具有儒家政治主张的人，未必穿儒服。穿儒服的人，未必了解儒家的政治主张。您如果一定认为不是这样的话，为什么不在国内发布命令：凡是不懂得儒道而穿儒服者，一律处以死罪。"

于是，鲁哀公就发布了这样的命令。过了五天，鲁国只出现一个男子穿着儒服站在君门旁，没有出现其他敢穿儒服的人。鲁哀公马上召见这位男子，并向他询问国事。不管鲁哀公提出什么问题，都难不倒这位男子。庄子见状，说："整个鲁国，儒者只有一个人罢了，能够说多吗？"

这则寓言讽刺了那些身穿儒服而不懂儒家之道的假儒士，说明了做事不能仅注重外表而忽视内在素质。

few mistakes; Then I balance three balls, and if they don't fall off, I know I will lose only one cicada in ten. At last, stacking five balls without falling will be as easy as picking cicadas on the ground. I stand up, and my body is no more than a broken stump, and my arm lifting the pole is like a branch of a rotten tree. Great as Heaven and Earth are, and multitudinous as things are, I don't notice any of them but only focus on the wings of cicadas; neither turning nor inclining to one side. I would not be distracted by any other thing in the world when I am sticking cicadas. How can I fail to do so?"

Confucius turned to his disciples and said, "Concentration without distraction means a high degree of cohesion of the spirit, and then you can practice your skills to the point of perfection. I'm afraid that's what the hunchback old man said."

This fable shows that if one can concentrate and study hard, he can practice his skills to the point of perfection.

45. All Wearing Confucian Dress in the State of Lu

This fable is from "Tian Zifang", *Zhuangzi*.

Zhuangzi visited Duke Ai of Lu, who told him, "At present, there are many scholars of the Confucian school in the state of Lu, but few scholars of your school." Zhuangzi responded, "There are few Confucians in the state of Lu." Duke Ai felt strange to hear that, so he retorted, "People in the state of Lu all wear the Confucian dress, and how can you say it few?" Zhuangzi replied, "I've heard that the Confucians who wear a domed hat know the changes of the opportune time of the heaven. People who wear square shoes know the terrain. If one ties jade Jue with five colored ribbons, he must be a man of determination. I don't think people with political views of Confucian school must wear Confucian dress. Instead, those who wear Confucian dress may not understand political views of Confucian school. If you don't think so, why don't you issue an order that those who do not understand Confucianism and yet still wear the Confucian dress will be sentenced to death?"

So Duke Ai issued such an order. After five days, there was only one man in Confucian dress standing beside the king's gate in the state of Lu. Duke Ai immediately summoned the man and asked him about state affairs. No matter what question Duke Ai asked, they could not defeat this man. Seeing this,

46. 弄水浸畦

这则寓言出自《庄子·天地》。"弄水浸畦"也称作"抱瓮灌畦""抱瓮灌园"或"抱瓮灌圃"。

孔子的弟子子贡去南方的楚国游玩,在回晋国的路上,经过汉水南岸时,看见一位老人正在经营菜园。

子贡见老人从开凿的通道下到井里,抱着一瓮水上来浇菜地,十分吃力,功效甚微,就对老人说:"这里有一种机械,一天可以浇一百畦菜地,用力少,效果好,您不想用吗?"

老人听了,扬起头来看了看子贡,说:"是什么样的机械?"

子贡回答说:"把木头凿成机关,后面重,前面轻,用它提水像引水一样,水会连续不断地涌出,它名叫桔槔。"

老人听了以后,十分生气,一下变了脸色,讥笑地说道:"我从老师那儿听说,有灵巧工具的人,一定有投机取巧的事情。有投机取巧事情的,一定有机变狡诈之心。机变的心存在于胸中,那么纯洁的心灵就不具备。纯洁的心灵不具备,思想就不会安定。思想不安定的人,是世道所不容。我不是不知道桔槔这种工具,我是耻于用它。"

庄子用这则寓言意在比喻古人淳朴的生活,现在多用来讽刺因循守旧、顽固不化,不思改进的人。

47. 白驹过隙

这则寓言出自《庄子·知北游》。

孔子向老子请教什么是大道。老子说:"大道是深奥神妙、难以言表的,我只能给你说个大概。人生于天地之间,就像骏马穿过一个狭窄的通道,瞬间而过罢了。人生的规律,就是自然而然地生,自然而然地死。人从没有形体变为有形体,再从有形体而变为消失形体。这是人所共知的东西,绝不是体悟大道的人所追求的道理,也不是人们所共同谈论的话题,体悟大道的人就不会去议论,议论的人就没有真正体悟大

Zhuangzi said, "There is only one Confucian in the whole state of Lu. Can you say many?"

This fable satirizes those false Confucians who wear Confucian dress but don't understand the way of Confucianism, and shows that we can't only pay attention to the appearance but ignore the internal quality.

46. Fetching Water to Water Fields

The fable is from "Heaven and Earth", *Zhuangzi*. It is also called "Carrying Jars to Water Fields", or "Carrying Jars to Water the Vegetable Garden".

Zigong, one disciple of Confucius, once traveled to a southern state of Chu. On his way back to Jin, when he was passing the south bank of the Han River, he saw an old man working in his vegetable garden.

Zigong saw the old man went down to the well through a tunnel, and fetched a jar of water up to water the fields. He had been working hard at it but by no means efficiently, so he told the old man, "There is a machine that can irrigate a hundred fields, demanding very little effort and producing excellent effect. Wouldn't you try this?"

The old man raised his head and looked at Zigong, "What kind of machine is it?"

Zigong replied, "Chisel the wood into a mechanism with a heavy back and light front. Using it to lift water is like diverting water which will gush out continuously. It's called Jugao (shadoof)."

After hearing this, the old man flushed with anger and said sarcastically, "I heard from my master that people who have smart tools must be opportunistic. Those who are opportunistic must be cunning. If the mind of cunning exists, then his mind is not purified any more. Without pure mind, one's thought will not be stable. People with unstable thoughts are not conforming to the Tao of the world. It's not that I don't know about Jugao, I'm just ashamed to use it."

Zhuangzi uses this fable to describe the simple life of the ancients. Now it is used to satirize those who are conservative, stubborn and do not want to improve.

47. A White Horse Passing Through a Crevice

This fable is from "Zhi Traveling North", *Zhuangzi*.

白驹过隙

A White Horse Passing Through a Crevice

道。十分张扬地寻找大道,倒不如真正地对大道有所体悟,巧舌善辩不如闭口不言。道不可能通过传言听到,希望听到传言,还不如塞耳不听,做到这些,才能真正懂得了玄妙的大道。"

这则寓言告诉我们,时间过得极快,就像白色的骏马飞快地从狭小的缝隙前越过一样。

48. 肘上生瘤

这则寓言出自《庄子·至乐》。

支离叔和滑介叔到杳冥昏暗的山上去游玩,这里是昆仑山的荒野之地,曾经是黄帝止步的地方。不一会儿,滑介叔的左肘上突然长出一个瘤。支离叔看他好像有点惊悚厌恶的样子,便问道:"你讨厌它吗?"滑介叔说:"不,我为什么讨厌它?人的生命,只不过是大自然假借的形骸。形骸上长出肿瘤,不过是形骸生长变化中的一些尘土和污垢罢了。生和死就像昼和夜一样是自然而平常的变化。况且我和您是来观察大自

Confucius consulted Laozi what is the Tao. Laozi said, "The Tao is profound and mysterious which cannot be expressed, so I can only give you a general idea. Life between Heaven and Earth is like a horse passing through a narrow passage in an instant. The law of life is naturally born and die. Men transform from no form to form, and then from form to form vanished. This is a well-known thing but not a reason pursued by people who understand the Tao, nor the topic that people talk about together. People who understand the great Tao will not talk about it, and people who talk about it will not really understand the great Tao. It's better to have a real understanding of the great Tao than to seek the Tao openly. It's better to keep silent than to be eloquent. It's impossible for Tao to be heard through rumors. If you want to hear Tao, you'd better not listen to the rumors. Only by doing this, can you really understand the great mysterious Tao."

This fable tells us that time flies like a white horse flying through a narrow crevice.

48. Tumors on the Elbow

This fable is from "Supreme Happiness" of *Zhuangzi*.

Zhili Shu and Huajie Shu went to the dark mountain to play. This was the wilderness of Kunlun Mountain, which used to be the place where the Yellow Emperor stopped by. After a while, a tumor suddenly appeared on Huajie Shu's elbow. Zhili Shu found Huajie Shu seemed to be a little frightened and disgusted, so he asked, "Do you hate it?"Huajie Shu said, "Not at all, why do I hate it?" Man's life is nothing but the body formed by nature. The tumor on the body is just some dust and dirt in the growth and change of the body. Life and death are just like day and night, which are all natural transformation of nature. Besides, you and I are here to observe the transformation of nature. Now that it has transformation on me, what else do I hate?"

Huajie Shu regarded the tumor on the elbow as a natural transformation. By this fable, Zhuangzi expresses his thought of letting nature take its course and being at ease with the situation. At the same time, it also warns future generations to be optimistic in the face of adversity.

然变化的,现在变化到了我身上,我还有什么厌恶的呢?"

滑介叔把肘上生瘤看作自然变化,安然处之。庄子借这则寓言,表达了他顺其自然、随遇而安的思想。同时也告诫后人,面对厄运,要以乐观的态度处之。

49. 庄子梦骷髅

这则寓言出自《庄子·至乐》。

庄子到楚国去,途中见到一个干枯的人头骨。庄子用马鞭从侧旁敲了敲,问道:"先生你是贪求生命、失却真理,因而成了这样的呢?还是你遇上了亡国的大事,遭受到杀戮而成了这样呢?还是有了不好的行为,担心给父母、妻儿子女留下耻辱,羞愧而死成了这样呢?还是你遭受寒冷、饥饿的灾祸而成了这样呢?还是你享尽天年而死去成了这样呢?"庄子说罢,拿过骷髅当作枕头枕着睡着了。

到了半夜,庄子梦见骷髅对他说:"听你刚才的谈话,你真像一个善于辩论的人。听你所说的那些话,全属于活人的拘累,人死了就没有这些忧虑了。你愿意听听人死后的快乐吗?"庄子说:"好。"骷髅说:"人死后,没有国君的统治,没有官吏的管辖;也没有四季的劳役,可以从容安逸地把天地的长久看作时令的流逝,即使南面为王的快乐,也不可能相比。"庄子不相信,说道:"我让司命来恢复你的形体,为你重新长出骨肉肌肤,使你和你的父母、妻子儿女、左右邻里和朋友故交重聚,你愿意吗?"骷髅皱着眉头,深感忧虑地说:"我怎么能抛弃这君王一样的快乐而再次遭受人世的劳苦呢?"

骷髅托梦给庄子,表达的是"生不如死"的命题。这是战国时期特定社会环境下的产物。面对恃强凌弱、战乱频繁的动荡社会,庄子从社会现实出发,揭露、批判了社会的不平等、不自由。

49. Zhuangzi Dreaming of a Skull

This fable is from "Supreme Happiness" of *Zhuangzi*.

On his way to the state of Chu, Zhuangzi saw a dried skull. Zhuangzi knocked on the side of the skull with his whip and asked, "Sir, let me guess how you became like this? Is it because you were greedy of your life and departed from the truth? Or did you encounter a great event of national subjugation and be killed? Or did you commit suicide with the guilt of bad behavior, worrying about leaving shame on your parents, wife and children? Or did you suffer from cold and hunger? Or did you live out the years Heaven gave and died like this?" Zhuangzi took the skull as a pillow and fell asleep.

It was midnight, Zhuangzi dreamed of the skull who talked with him, "Look at the conversation you just had. You look so much like a good debater. Look at what you have said. It's all about the bondage of the living. When a man dies, there will be no worries like that. Would you like to hear about the happiness after death?" Zhuangzi replied, "Ok." The skull said, "After death, there is no monarch's rule, no official's jurisdiction; There is no change of four seasons. Ease and comfort are the permanent state of Heaven and Earth. Thus even the happiness of being a king in the South cannot be compared with it. Zhuangzi didn't believe it and said, "I'll ask Siming to restore your body, to grow flesh and blood for you, and to reunite you with your parents, your wife and children, your neighbors and friends. Will you?" The skull frowned and said anxiously, "How can I abandon the pleasure of a king and suffer the hardships of the world again?"

The skull entrusted a dream to Zhuangzi to express the proposition that "life is not as good as death". This idea is rooted in the specific social environment in the Warring States period. Facing the turbulent society of bullying and frequent wars, Zhuangzi exposed and criticized the inequality and lack of freedom of the society from the social reality.

50. 津人操舟

这则寓言出自《庄子·达生》。

颜渊问孔子："我曾经在觞深渡口过渡，摆渡人驾船的技巧实在神妙。我问摆渡人：'驾船可以学习吗？'他说：'可以的。善于游泳的人很快就能学会。假如是善于潜水的人，即使不曾见到船，也会熟练轻巧地驾驶船。'我再问他驾船的道理，他却不再回答我。请问他的话说的是什么意思呢？"

孔子回答说："善于游泳的人很快就能学会驾船，这是因为他们熟悉水性，而能处之自然。至于那善于潜水的人，虽不曾见到过船就能熟练地驾驶船，是因为他们眼里的深渊就像是陆地上的高地，看待船翻犹如车子倒退一样。船的覆没和车的倒退等各种危险情况，出现在他们眼前却都不能扰乱他们的内心，如果内心若无其事，那么他们到哪里不会从容自得呢？用瓦器作为赌注的人，内心坦然而格外技高；用金属带钩作为赌注的人，便会心存疑惧；用黄金作为赌注的人，则头脑发昏，内心迷乱。赌博的技巧本是一样的，但如果有所顾惜，那就是以身外之物为重的缘故。大凡对外物看得太重的人，其内心世界一定笨拙。"

庄子借孔子与弟子颜渊的对话，说明做事情如果有心理负担，计较利害得失，往往不能成功。

50. A Ferryman Sailing

This fable is from "Full Understanding of Life" of *Zhuangzi*.

Yan Yuan asked Confucius, "I used to ferry at Shangshen ferry, and the ferryman's skill in sailing is really wonderful. I asked the ferryman, 'Can sailing be learned?' He said, 'Yes. Those who are good at swimming will soon learn it. If you are good at diving, even if you have never seen a boat, you will also skillfully and deftly steer it.' I continued to ask him the reason for sailing, but he didn't answer me anymore. What does he mean by that?"

Confucius replied, "People who are good at swimming will soon learn to sail because they are familiar with the nature of water and can live in it naturally. As for those who are good at diving, although they have never seen a boat before, they can skillfully steer it because the abyss in their eyes is like a highland on land, and the overturning of a boat is like a car going backwards. All kinds of dangerous situations, such as the wreck of the ship and the retrogression of the car, can't disturb their minds when they appear in front of them. If there is nothing in their minds, no matter where they go, they can take their time and be complacent. Taking gambling as an example, if one bet with a piece of cheap pottery, he would put forth all his skill in winning without scruple ; If one bet with metal buckles, the prize be a buckle of brass, he would shoot timorously; the one who gambles on gold will be confused and shoots as if he were blind. The skill of gambling is the same, but there are scruples, it is because we pay much attention to external things out of our body. The man who values external things too much must be clumsy."

Zhuangzi uses the dialogue between Confucius and his disciple Yan Yuan to explain that if one has psychological burden and cares about gain and loss, he can't succeed.

附录1：庄子思想导图

- 庄子
  - 战国道家学派 —— 继承发展老子思想，世人称"老庄"
  - 《庄子》
    - 内篇 —— 逍遥游　齐物论　养生主　人间世　德充符　大宗师　应帝王
    - 外篇 —— 骈拇　马蹄　胠箧　在宥　天地　天运　刻意　缮性　秋水　至乐　田子方　知北游
    - 杂篇 —— 庚桑楚　徐无鬼　则阳　外物　寓言　让王　盗跖　说剑　渔父　列御寇　天下
  - 寓言 —— 庄周梦蝶　邯郸学步　越俎代庖　朝三暮四
              庖丁解牛　东施效颦　螳螂捕蝉　运斤成风
  - 思想 —— 无为而治　逍遥游　齐物论
  - 经典语句
    - 吾生也有涯，而知也无涯。以有涯随无涯，殆已
    - 人生天地之间，若白驹之过隙，污染而已
    - 世俗之人，皆喜人之同乎己，而恶人之异于己也
    - 哀莫大于心死，而人死亦次之
    - 井蛙不可以语于海，夏虫不可以语于冰
    - 狗不以善吠为良，人不以善言为贤
    - 好面誉人者，亦好背而毁之
    - 谋无主则困，事无备则废
    - 不精不诚，不能动人
    - 独与天地精神往来，而不敖倪于万物

Appendix 1: Mind Map of Zhuangzi's Thoughts

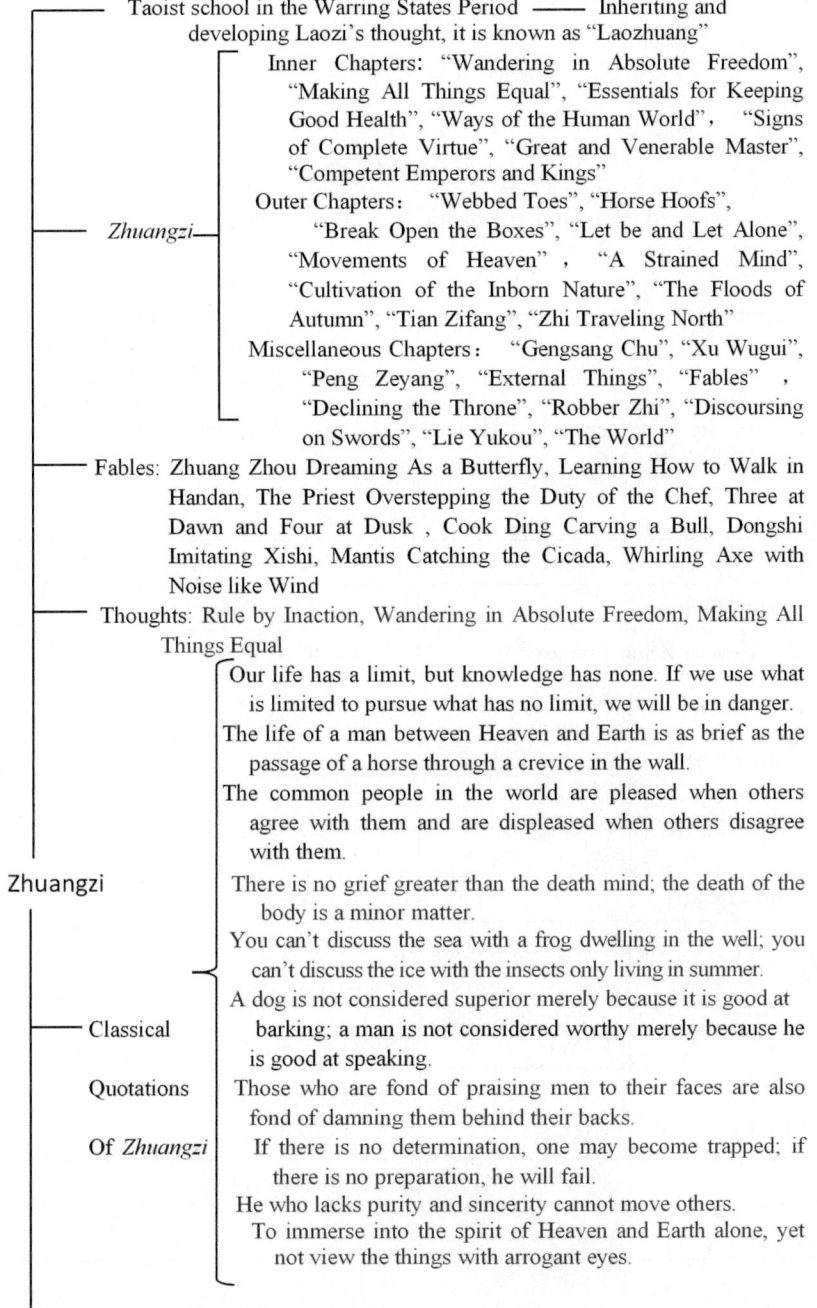

- Zhuangzi
  - Taoist school in the Warring States Period —— Inheriting and developing Laozi's thought, it is known as "Laozhuang"
  - Zhuangzi
    - Inner Chapters: "Wandering in Absolute Freedom", "Making All Things Equal", "Essentials for Keeping Good Health", "Ways of the Human World", "Signs of Complete Virtue", "Great and Venerable Master", "Competent Emperors and Kings"
    - Outer Chapters: "Webbed Toes", "Horse Hoofs", "Break Open the Boxes", "Let be and Let Alone", "Movements of Heaven", "A Strained Mind", "Cultivation of the Inborn Nature", "The Floods of Autumn", "Tian Zifang", "Zhi Traveling North"
    - Miscellaneous Chapters: "Gengsang Chu", "Xu Wugui", "Peng Zeyang", "External Things", "Fables", "Declining the Throne", "Robber Zhi", "Discoursing on Swords", "Lie Yukou", "The World"
  - Fables: Zhuang Zhou Dreaming As a Butterfly, Learning How to Walk in Handan, The Priest Overstepping the Duty of the Chef, Three at Dawn and Four at Dusk, Cook Ding Carving a Bull, Dongshi Imitating Xishi, Mantis Catching the Cicada, Whirling Axe with Noise like Wind
  - Thoughts: Rule by Inaction, Wandering in Absolute Freedom, Making All Things Equal
  - Classical Quotations Of *Zhuangzi*
    - Our life has a limit, but knowledge has none. If we use what is limited to pursue what has no limit, we will be in danger.
    - The life of a man between Heaven and Earth is as brief as the passage of a horse through a crevice in the wall.
    - The common people in the world are pleased when others agree with them and are displeased when others disagree with them.
    - There is no grief greater than the death mind; the death of the body is a minor matter.
    - You can't discuss the sea with a frog dwelling in the well; you can't discuss the ice with the insects only living in summer.
    - A dog is not considered superior merely because it is good at barking; a man is not considered worthy merely because he is good at speaking.
    - Those who are fond of praising men to their faces are also fond of damning them behind their backs.
    - If there is no determination, one may become trapped; if there is no preparation, he will fail.
    - He who lacks purity and sincerity cannot move others.
    - To immerse into the spirit of Heaven and Earth alone, yet not view the things with arrogant eyes.

附录2：中国历史年代简表
Appendix2: A Brief Chronology of Chinese History

中国历史年代简表
A Brief Chronology of Chinese History

五帝时代 Period of the Five Legendary Rulers c. 2600 BC-c. 2070 BC		黄帝 Huangdi (Yellow Emperor)
		颛顼 Zhuanxu
		帝喾 Diku (Emperor Ku)
		尧 Yao
		舜 Shun
夏 Xia Dynasty		c. 2070 BC-c. 1600 BC
商 Shang Dynasty		c. 1600 BC-c. 1046 BC
西周 Western Zhou Dynasty		c. 1046 BC-c. 771 BC
东周 Eastern Zhou Dynasty 770 BC-256 BC	春秋 Spring and Autumn Period	770 BC-476 BC
	战国 Warring States Period	475 BC-221 BC
秦 Qin Dynasty		221 BC-206 BC
汉 Han Dynasty 206 BC-220 AD	西汉 Western Han	206 BC-25 AD
	东汉 Eastern Han	25 AD-220 AD
三国 Three Kingdoms 220 AD-280 AD	魏 Wei	220 AD-265 AD
	蜀汉 Shu Han	221 AD-263 AD
	吴 Wu	222 AD-280 AD
晋 Jin Dynasty 265 AD-420 AD	西晋 Western Jin	265 AD-317 AD
	东晋 Eastern Jin	317 AD-420 AD

续表 Continued Table

南北朝 Southern and Northern Dynasties 420 AD-589 AD	南朝 Southern Dynasties	宋 Song	420 AD-479 AD
		齐 Qi	479 AD-502 AD
		梁 Liang	502 AD-557 AD
		陈 Chen	557 AD-589 AD
	北朝 Northern Dynasties	北魏 Northern Wei	386 AD-534 AD
		东魏 Eastern Wei	534 AD-550 AD
		北齐 Northern Qi	550 AD-577 AD
		西魏 Western Wei	535 AD-556 AD
		北周 Northern Zhou	557 AD-581 AD
隋 Sui Dynasty			581 AD-618 AD
唐 Tang Dynasty			618 AD-907 AD
五代十国 Five Dynasties and Ten States	五代 Five Dynasties 907 AD-960 AD	后梁 Later Liang	907 AD-923 AD
		后唐 Later Tang	923 AD-936 AD
		后晋 Later Jin	936 AD-947 AD
		后汉 Later Han	947 AD-950 AD
		后周 Later Zhou	951 AD-960 AD
	十国 Ten States 902 AD-979 AD	北汉 Northern Han	951 AD-979 AD
		吴 Wu	902 AD-937 AD
		吴越 Wuyue	907 AD-978 AD
		闽 Min	909 AD-945 AD
		南汉 Southern Han	917 AD-971 AD
		荆南（又称"南平"）Jingnan (Nanping)	924 AD-963 AD
		楚 Chu	927 AD-951 AD
		南唐 Southern Tang	937 AD-975 AD
		前蜀 Former Shu	907 AD-925 AD
		后蜀 Later Shu	934 AD-965 AD

续表 Continued Table

宋 Song Dynasty 960 AD-1279 AD	北宋 Northern Song	960 AD-1127 AD
	南宋 Southern Song	1127 AD-1279 AD
辽 Liao (契丹 Qidan/Khitan)	907 AD-1125 AD	
西夏 Xixia (Tangut)	1038 AD-1227 AD	
金 Jin	1115 AD-1234 AD	
元 Yuan Dynasty	1206 AD-1368 AD	
明 Ming Dynasty	1368 AD-1644 AD	
清 Qing Dynasty	1616 AD-1911 AD	
中华民国 Republic of China	1912 AD-1949 AD	
中华人民共和国 People's Republic of China	1949 AD-	

后　记

庄子是战国时期宋国蒙（今河南商丘）人，死后葬在今河南省民权县老颜集乡唐庄村，主要生活在以商丘为中心的古代河南、山东、安徽这一交界地带的黄河文明的发源地，他的故事在这片钟灵毓秀的沃土上广为流传。

《庄子》是中国最主要的元典文化之一。既是一部伟大的哲学著作，也是一部价值很高的文学著作。阅读《庄子》，会给我们带来不一样的感受，他的"无为"与"无己"，独与天地精神往来，逍遥自在，与世间万物一体的思想，与看重人的社会属性、带有强烈的政治伦理色彩的儒家学说相比，自有另外一番天地。重视人的自然本性，关怀人的生命和精神，对生命的热爱和珍惜，强烈的个性色彩……所有这些，对中国人独立人格的养成，起着不可忽视的作用。

在写作《中华源·河南故事·庄子》的过程中，我们也深深地感受到了《庄子》内容的丰厚与博大，感到了对其博大精深思想把握的艰难。因而，不得不一遍一遍地翻检《庄子》的不同注本，学习、研究大家的不同解读，梳理庄子的出生地、工作地、埋葬地的种种说法，以至于耗时很多，数易其稿。

本书作为"翻译河南"工程的重要部分，编写工作得到了河南省政府外事办公室领导的高度重视和支持，商丘师范学院校领导、国际交流处、党政办公室的同人给予了大力支持。在此一并表示感谢。

仰之弥高，钻之弥坚。庄子思想博大精深，我们心向往之，但我们对《庄子》及各家注说的理解可能还不到位，加上时间仓促，内容难免有纰漏之处，敬请广大读者谅解。

编写组
2021年1月22日

Postscript

Zhuangzi was born in Meng, the state of Song (now Shangqiu, Henan Province) during the Warring States period. He was buried in Tangzhuang Village, Laoyanji Township, Minquan County, Henan Province. Thus, it is widely acknowledged that Zhuangzi mainly lived in the border region of ancient Henan, Shandong and Anhui , which is ,with Shangqiu City as its center, the birthplaces of the Yellow River civilization. So, his story is inseparable from this piece of land full of nature bestows.

Zhuangzi is one of the most important original cultures in China. It is not only a great philosophical work, but also a valuable literary work. Reading *Zhuangzi* will bring us distinct feelings. His thoughts of "Inaction" and "No Self", immersing into the spirit of Heaven and Earth alone, Absolute Freedom, and the idea of "taking all things in the world as equal" , integrating with all things in the world, are quite unique and different from Confucianism, which values the social attributes of human beings and has a strong political and ethical color. Attaching importance to human nature, caring for human life and spirit, loving and cherishing life, a unique personality… all these play an important role in the development of Chinese independent character.

In the process of writing this book of *Chinese Civilization Stories from Henan Zhuangzi* , we are deeply impressed by the rich and broad content of *Zhuangzi*, and the difficulty of handling the material appropriately. We have to repeatedly review the different annotations of *Zhuangzi*, understand and study the different interpretations of the masters and experts, and sort out the various statements of Zhuangzi's birthplace, work place and burial place, so that it takes a lot of time to revise the manuscript.

As an important part of the "Translating Henan" project, the compilation of this book has been highly valued and supported by leaders from the Foreign Affairs Office of CPC Committee of Henan Province, And the leaders of Shangqiu Normal University, colleagues from the International Exchange Office and the Office of Party and Government Affairs have given strong support. We are grateful to all of them here.

The more respected, the more sublime it seemed; the harder we studied on it, the more profound and abstruse the meaning became. Zhuangzi's thought is broad and profound, and we are eager to pursue it. However, our understanding of *Zhuangzi* and other commentaries of it may not be in place. In addition, due to the limit of time, the book is inevitably with some flaws. Criticisms from the readers are welcome.

Writing group
January 22, 2021